AN IDENTIFICATION
GUIDE TO
CAT
BREEDS

JILL CARAVAN

AN IDENTIFICATION
GUIDE TO
CAT
BREEDS

JILL CARAVAN

GALLERY BOOKS
An imprint of W.H. Smith Publishers Inc.
112 Madison Avenue
New York, New York 10016

A QUINTET BOOK
produced for
GALLERY BOOKS
An imprint of W. H. Smith Publishers Inc.
112 Madison Avenue
New York, New York 10016

ISBN 0–8317–4819–2

This book was designed and produced by
Quintet Publishing Limited
6 Blundell Street
London N7 9BH

Creative Director: *Terry Jeavons*
Art Director: *Ian Hunt*
Designer: *Wayne Blades*
Project Editor: *Sally Harper*
Editor: *Michele Staple*
Illustrator: *Amanda Evans*

Typeset in Great Britain by
Central Southern Typesetters, Eastbourne
Manufactured in Hong Kong by
Regent Publishing Services Limited
Printed in Singapore by Tien Wah Press (Pte) Ltd.

CONTENTS

AN INTRODUCTION TO THE CAT

EVOLUTION AND HISTORY

Persians have the look and feel of elegance and fine living. The Norwegian Forest Cat is reminiscent of the wild, untamed world. The Ragdoll is an adorable, docile animal, and the Siamese exudes the world of the mystical. As different as they are, these four of the hundred-plus breeds of domestic cat that exist in the world today are all descendants of the same ancestor.

The first cat was among the carnivores known as miacids that evolved some 50 million years ago from the first mammals.

BELOW LEFT: Today's different breeds of domestic cat are partly the result of man's early travels and explorations. The Siamese, for example, is probably the descendant of a few hundred cats taken from Egypt to Siam thousands of years ago.

cannot fully retract; and *Felis*, which includes smaller cats such as the domestic cat that have a rigid hyoid bone and cannot roar. The domestic cat, *Felis catus*, is probably descended from two species: *F. sylvestris* (European Wildcat) and *F. libyca* (African Wildcat).

The first tamed cats were used to protect grain from rats in ancient Egypt around 3000 BC, and came to be loved as companions and worshipped as gods. It became a crime to hurt or kill them. Cats were domesticated in the Far East, too, probably between 2000 BC and AD 400. Approximately 400 cats were eventually taken to Siam (Thailand) from Egypt by grain merchants, and those cats are thought to have been the ancestors of today's Siamese. The earliest record of domestic cats in Great Britain that has been discovered so

ABOVE RIGHT: Some of the earliest domestic cats to arrive in America were British Shorthairs or European Shorthairs who made the seventeenth-century voyage with the Pilgrims.

The first mammals, in turn, had sprung from a group of meat-eating reptiles called therapsids about 200 million years ago. The oldest-known fossil similar to today's cats is about 12 million years old.

Felidae is the family name for all cats, and is divided into three genera: *Panthera*, which includes big cats such as lions and tigers that have a small hyoid bone at the base of their tongue; *Acinonyx*, represented only by the cheetah, which has claws that

far goes back to AD 936, when a law was enacted to protect them.

Although cats were revered early in their domestication, their position had changed by the Middle Ages. Because they had not been or were just being domesticated at the time it was written, cats were never mentioned in the Bible. The Christian Church disliked their connections with pagan cults, including the superstition that witches assumed their form, and waged

LEFT: T*he domestic cat of today represents one of three directions in which the cat family that originated about 12 million years ago has evolved.*

a campaign against them. At the height of the tirade, cats were often burned alive by Christians.

But as their usefulness became evident, they became better known for their skill against rodents than for being agents of evil. In the seventeenth century, cats of the traditional tabby pattern were taken by the Pilgrims to America. (Today, almost half the cats in the Boston area have that same tabby pattern, and the ranges of the original toms can be determined by cats with coats of that pattern). By the eighteenth century, they were again common in households.

The concept of breeds began in the mid-nineteenth century, and by the end of the century, early pedigree breeds were exhibited at the first cat shows. But to understand breeds, it is first necessary to understand the basic anatomy and behaviour of the cat.

ANATOMY AND CHARACTERISTICS

Your gentle little Fluffy may not look very fierce curled up on your couch, but she has a digestive tract designed for meat-eating, and the physique and instincts of a hunting animal (one that stalks, pounces and tears). Although dogs and cats are both carnivores, cats are more adapted to the role of hunter. In general, wild dogs hunt in packs, while most cats hunt alone. Because dogs have been companions to humans for so long, they have lost much of their resemblance to their wolf-like ancestors. But cats still retain the physique and temperament of their wild relatives.

The average cat weighs about 4 kg (9 lb), is 30 cm (12 in) high at the shoulder, and about 80 cm (31 in) long from head to tip of tail. Its 245 bones and 517 muscles are formed into one of three basic cat shapes:

● cobby – flat face, short legs, wide shoulders and hind, and short, round head;
● muscular – medium legs, shoulders and hind, with slightly round head; and
● lithe – long thin legs, narrow shoulders and hind, and long, wedge-shaped head.

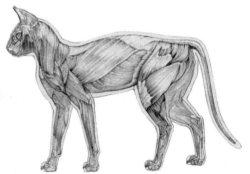

Cats' vertebrae are more loosely connected than are humans', making their spines very flexible – a big plus for squeezing through tiny spaces. This also enables the cat to arch its back. They are good climbers, thanks to the strong muscles in their backs and legs, and the curved claws on their paws. Unfortunately, they are not as adept at climbing down, because their claws curve the wrong way and their powerful muscles aren't adapted to holding back the body's weight. That is why

BELOW: **D**uring the Middle Ages, domestic cats were nearly wiped out in Europe as the Christian Church waged war on them because of the feline's supposed connection with pagan rituals and witches. Black cats were particularly despised.

FAR RIGHT: **F**eline muscles combine strength with flexibility. The cat's skeleton is held together by more than 500 muscles (top). Of all these muscles, the strongest are in the neck and shoulders, and in the hind legs and lumbar region (bottom).

RIGHT: **T**he Persian displays the cobby body type, which incorporates wide shoulders and hind, short legs, and a short, round head. Other types are muscular and lithe.

LEFT: The design of the cat's face and eyes gives the feline a much larger field of vision than that of humans. It's a typical characteristic of a predatory animal.

LEFT: Cats are good climbers, although their claws and muscles are better adapted for moving up rather than down.

cats sometimes seem inept at coming down a tree once they have climbed up.

Although many cats are wanderers, they don't spend a great deal of time walking. As runners, they are better at short distances than long. When they run, they extend their legs completely in the air, then bring them down and thrust themselves forward from both back feet at once. Their feet are digitigrade (walking on the ends of their toes), as opposed to plantigrade (walking flat on the paw bones), and their forepaws have five toe pads, five claws and two large pads. The fifth claw acts like a thumb, for grasping. The hind paw has four toe pads, four claws and one large pad.

As efficient as the limbs are, it is a myth that cats can jump from high places and always land on all fours. But they can do almost anything connected with their senses. Cats have a greater field of vision than ours, allowing them to make accurate judgements in various terrains: 120 degrees of binocular (straight-ahead) vision,

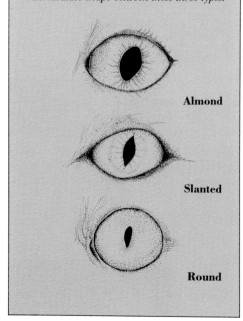

FELINE EYE SHAPES

One of the primary characteristics that distinguish one breed from another is eye shape. The three basic shapes are almond, slanted and round (shown below). Many cats' eyes are of an intermediate shape between these three types.

Almond

Slanted

Round

COLOURS OF EYES

Each breed and variety of cat has a permitted eye colour or a range of colours, as set down by the governing cat organizations. The pupil is generally black; the coloured area is called the iris. Irises may even vary in colour within an individual cat, as is the case with Odd-Eyed Whites.

RIGHT: **C**ats have more than three times as many scent cells in their nasal cavities as humans, giving them an excellent sense of smell.

plus 80 degrees of monocular vision on each side, making a total of 280 degrees. A curious membrane at the back of the eye called the tapetum lucidum houses a special light-conserving mechanism that enables cats to make the most of dim light. At night, the pupil opens wide to catch any available light, causing the tapetum to glow in the dark. In bright light, the pupil narrows to a slit. When cats are ill, a greyish membrane called a 'haw' (third eyelid) extends from the eye's edge to protect and moisten the eye.

While cats' eyes come in a rainbow of colours – greens, blues, golds – colour is not all that important to cats. Tests have shown that cats can distinguish between various colours, but they don't really need to be aware of them. Being able to detect movement is much more important. People sometimes think that cats are psychic because they seem to be able to detect disturbances long before they happen. In reality, they just hear things before we do and things that we cannot hear because of the pitch. Cats can perceive high-frequency sounds up to about 65 kHz (65,000 cycles per second). Humans hear up to about 20 kHz.

In general, the size of the ear is indicative of the origin of the breed. Ears are an important means of heat loss, and so larger ears would indicate temperate to tropical

origins, where they could function as a cooling mechanism. Small ears, like those of Persians, support the theory of a more northerly origin. Possibly because of their well-developed sense of balance, for which the ears are partly responsible, cats do not usually suffer from motion sickness.

The nose and mouth are very closely linked for a cat's sense of smell and taste. A cat's nasal cavity is filled with bony plates called turbinals that increase the surface area for smelling. Despite the small size of the head, a cat has about 60 million scent cells, compared with the 5-20 million present in humans.

Besides its nose, the cat has another odour-sensing organ in the roof of its mouth, called a Jacobson's organ (or flehmen). It is not linked to the same part of the brain as the olfactory nerves, but to the hypothalamus, providing motivation for feeding and sexual behaviour. When the animal uses its Jacobson's organ, we say it flehms, which involves inhaling while holding its breath, rolling back its lip and wrinkling its nose.

GESTURE AND EXPRESSION

Feline postures show much about the mood of a cat. (A) A content cat has upright ears, relaxed whiskers and a calm pose. (B) Anger is shown with raised fur on the spine, bristling whiskers, arched back and ears pulled back. (C) The dominant cat in a confrontation is in a higher position; its ears will be slightly back, its body held sideways and mouth held open.

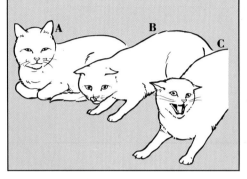

TOP: **T**he experts disagree over the source of the cat's purring, but cat owners know what causes it and that's all that matters.

CENTRE: **T**he 16-18 hours of sleep that a cat needs every day are generally accomplished in a soft, warm area that is free of traffic and distractions. However, sometimes any nice sunny spot will do.

BOTTOM: **W**ithin their territories, be that totally indoors or out, cats will establish their favoured spots for their daily activities, such as sleeping, playing, hunting, eating and relieving themselves.

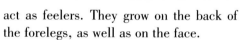

Also in the mouth are the cat's 30 teeth (including four canines), which serve to kill and then tear up fresh prey. The rough surface of the tongue which is loaded with sensory detectors for temperature and taste, is also useful for cleaning fur. Cats are able to taste sour, salt, bitter, sweet and water, but sweetness is not very important to them.

A cat's sense of touch involves its fur and skin, as well as its whiskers. In practical terms, both fur and whiskers are extensions of the skin. The skin includes a great number of 'touch spots' that are more sensitive than the areas around them. On the back of the neck, the skin is very thick and loose, suggesting that cats have not only been hunters but have been hunted themselves. Loose skin makes it easier for animals to squirm away from their captors. The loose skin also helps them work their way through precarious areas.

Fur does not have to actually touch something to feel it. Air flow caused by or bouncing off an object can be enough to alert a cat. But as sensitive as cats are to touch, they are not nearly as sensitive to temperature. Cats are not well adapted to cold or wet weather because they lack the protective layer of fat that dogs have. Whereas humans start to feel pain when touching something at about 44°C (112°F) cats don't notice it until about 51°C (124°F). Fortunately, cat's noses, snouts and upper lips are extremely sensitive to temperature changes. Whiskers, too, called 'vibrissae',

act as feelers. They grow on the back of the forelegs, as well as on the face.

At the cat's other end is the tail, a flexible extension of the spine that is just one of the many ways that cats convey their feelings. The tail whips up if the cat is threatening, stands upright and twitches if the cat is alert, and swishes low and close if the cat is aggressive. A raised, still tail

LEFT: F*ace and body language is a major means of communication for cats, both among themselves and with other species such as humans.*

is the sign of a friendly cat; an arched, bristled tail, a defensive cat; a thumping tail, a submissive cat. These tail signals are accompanied by signals from the ears, eyes, back and other body parts to convey a variety of feelings and messages.

An aggressive cat also has pricked ears held slightly back, smooth fur, narrow pupils, bristled whiskers and an open mouth. A defensive cat holds its ears back and sideways, bristles its fur and whiskers, arches its back, turns its body sideways, dilates its pupils and holds its mouth open. A submissive cat flattens its ears, fur and whiskers, cringes, dilates its pupils and holds its mouth open. A contented cat sits with eyes half-closed, maybe purring.

There are different schools of thought as to the source of purring. Some scientists think it's from turbulence in the main vein of the heart, caused when cats arch their backs. The blood vibrates, creating sounds that resonate in the sinuses. The more common theory on purring, however, is vibrations of membranes, called false vocal cords, located near the vocal cords.

Some experts say cats actually use consonants and vowels, and even diphthongs and a triphthong, to produce word-like sounds that convey feelings of anger, warning, excitement, concern, pain and sexuality. Along with these, cats are

RIGHT: Unlike dogs, cats remember only those 'tricks' that continue to have some direct benefit to them.

BELOW: Hunting ability and desire vary among cats in the same manner that different abilities and desires vary among humans. Much depends on the early training that the individual cat received from its mother.

ABOVE: Cats' brains require a constant flow of stimulation from their environment. This is a necessary condition for a growing and developing kitten to continue as a fully functioning adult.

gather. With these community territories come hierarchies, in which every cat has a position. The toughest tom cat becomes the most powerful. Females are organized by their achievements as mothers. The choicest spot in the territory – a soft, warm area, free of traffic and distractions – is chosen for the 16 to 18 hours a day that cats spend sleeping. But even though cats seem to be in another world during these sleep periods, their senses are alert for incoming stimuli, and their brains are almost as active as when they are awake.

Those same senses are even more cognizant during a cat's waking hours, especially if it is in the mood for hunting. In domestic cats, hunting is not necessarily for food, but more for sport. In fact, some cats don't immediately kill what they catch, preferring to play with their prey first. Even when cats look like they are just being curious about movements or objects, they are actually using their curiosity to fulfil their instinctive 'need' for food. This inborn curiosity, coupled with their innate cautiousness, is a manifestation of their high intelligence. Many other animals are incapable of suspecting danger or exploring just for the experience.

A cat's brain is able to process a continuous flow of stimuli from its environment and, in fact, needs that stimulation. Kittens whose senses are deprived from an early age actually grow up to function abnormally, and adult cats who are later deprived lose some brain activity and ability. As most human parents would affirm, the most intelligent offspring are those provided with an interesting and challenging environment. With cats, gentle handling and amusing play are the keys.

A cat's brain also has a capacity for memory, usually selective, based on the cat's needs. It remembers where it lives and what it likes to do, and it may remember some 'tricks' if the retention is beneficial.

known for meowing, when they wish to convey discontent or some need; gurgling; screeching; caterwauling; hissing; growling; tooth-chattering, when cats see prey but cannot reach it, and moving their mouths as if they already had it.

Another more subtle way cats communicate is by scent glands located on the tail, forehead, side of the mouth, chin and anus. Cats spread scents called pheromones to establish territory, and recognize each other by smelling these places. Male cats also spray urine to place scents and establish their 'turf', or territory. Turf is also important to those cats that don't seem territorial. Even house cats have favourite spots inside for eating, sleeping, urinating, defecating, playing and hunting. When cats share areas with other cats, the territory is joint property.

For cats who interact with others in a neighbourhood, there may be common, as well as individual, areas where they

BREEDS AND SHOWS

Most cats you see around the neighbourhood are basic non-pedigree cats, commonly called moggies. There are, however, approximately a hundred breeds classified by various organizations throughout the world. Differences among breeds include length and type of coat, colour, markings and body form.

The notion of breeds began in the nineteenth century. Originally breeders focused on cats in Great Britain, but soon more intriguing-looking cats — Persians and Siamese — were imported. By the end of the century, there were cat shows to display those early pedigree breeds. The first official competition was held in 1871 at the Crystal Palace in London (although there are records of one as long ago as 1598). That first nineteenth-century show was for British Shorthair and Persian types. The first American show was held around the same time in New England for the Maine Coon breed.

Today, breeds are generally divided into two categories: longhairs and shorthairs. Longhaired cats are extremely attractive because of their hair. Unfortunately, because of it they moult (shed) all year round and require daily grooming to prevent matting. Most longhairs are known as Persian. Persians have a cobby (sturdy and rounded) body with a round face and head, short thick legs, a short nose and large, round eyes. The other features these cats have in common is an exceptionally full coat. It is called a double coat because it has both a soft, woolly undercoat and a slightly longer,

BELOW: Non-pedigree cats, *the majority of all domestic and feral cats today, are called moggies.*

ABOVE: **M**oggie cats, although lacking the blue-blood ancestry of many of the true breeds, are permitted in many shows.

coarser coat up to 11.5 cm (4.5 in) long. The longhaired cats that are not Persian come from cold climates where a long coat is useful. Their coats are not usually as woolly or as full as those of Persians. They are also slimmer, longer and easier to groom.

Short hair is far more common because the genes for short hair are dominant over those for long hair. Unlike long hair, a short coat is generally easy to care for: simpler to clean, it won't tangle, and is

less likely to cause hairballs or blockages within the digestive system. It also has health advantages, as wounds can be more easily cared for and parasites can be caught earlier.

In Great Britain, classification is decided by the Governing Council of the Cat Fancy (GCCF) and the Cat Association. In the United States of America, there are several organizations, including the American Cat Association (the oldest), the Cat Fanciers' Association (the largest),

COAT TYPES IN DIFFERENT BREEDS

A cat's coat may consist of three hair types:
top coat or guard hairs
bristly awn hairs
undercoat or down hairs

Persian (Longhair): *Dense with long guard hairs of up to 12.5cm (5in) and thick down hairs.*

Angora: *Finer than the Persian; both guard and down hairs are very long.*

Maine Coon: *Down and guard hairs are long, like the Persian, but shaggy and uneven.*

Devon Rex: *Guard, awn and down hairs all very curly and short.*

British Shorthair: *Sparse awn hairs with guard hairs of about 4.5cm (2in).*

Sphynx: *No guard or awn hairs; just a few down hairs on face, legs and tail.*

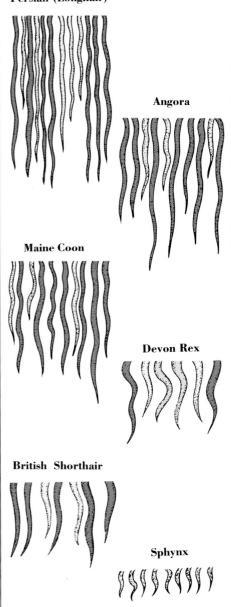

Persian (Longhair)

Angora

Maine Coon

Devon Rex

British Shorthair

Sphynx

COAT TIPPING

Bands of colour on each hair in a cat's coat give different shading effects. Tipping may appear only at the end of the hair or go right down to the root; it may also consist of bands of colour. The main types are (A) ticked; (B) smoke; (C) shaded; (D) shell; and (E) untipped.

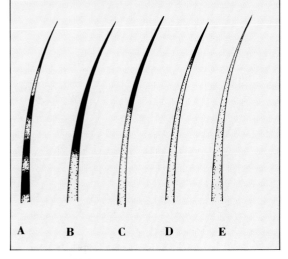

A **B** **C** **D** **E**

the American Cat Fanciers' Association, the Cat Fanciers' Federation, the Crown Cat Fanciers' Federation and the International Cat Association. The Canadian Cat Association is the governing body for Canada. The Federation Internationale Feline de L'Europe is the largest in continental Europe. Cat organizations generally establish standards for all breeds, provide for registration of pedigrees and transfers of ownership, and approve show dates (addresses of major organizations are listed on pages 90 and 91).

Whether your cat is Persian – the most popular breed in the cat fancy (the world of cat breeding and showing) – or something of less blue-blood ancestry, you can enjoy and compete in cat shows. Many cat clubs provide for the showing of non-pedigreed cats or crossbreeds that cannot be placed in a specific breed class. To enter, contact the sponsoring organization for an entry form. You will also receive show rules, which are laid down to ensure fairness and protect the interests of the cat. For example, usually after showing, you must wait at least a week before exhibiting again. Another rule usually prohibits the use of anything that could alter the cat's appearance. These rules vary between countries and even between different regions and organizations, so be sure to check.

The usual procedure is to enter your cat or kitten in one basic colour class for its

ABOVE: **T**he fact that more cats are shorthaired reflects the dominance of shorthair genes over those for longhair.

RIGHT: **E**very breed of cat
has its own standard of points,
against which each individual
cat is evaluated.

RIGHT: **S**how cats need
to be accustomed to being
handled, particularly at arm's
length.

breed according to its status, ie Open, Champion or Grand Champion. It will be judged in this class, as well as in every all-breed and speciality competition for which it is eligible. On show day, you'll need the following equipment and supplies: travelling container, litter pan, feeding dish, food, water bowl, water bottle, show blanket, grooming tools, favourite toy, vaccination certificates and other paperwork that the particular show requires.

The first thing that happens on show day is called 'vetting-in' – a thorough health check by a veterinarian. If for some reason – fleas, soreness, running nose – the cat fails the examination, you will be

disqualified and forfeit your entry fee. Make sure your cat is used to travelling by car; if it has symptoms of motion sickness, it may be disqualified.

After vetting-in, you can take your cat to its pen – a metal cage displaying the cat's show entry number. (Because your cat will need to be penned during much of the show, you should accustom it to being penned. Begin by penning it for a few minutes a day, and progressively lengthen the time.) Take some time to arrange the pen for comfort and eye appeal. Many owners put a lot of effort into assuring that the decoration highlights the cat's colouring. (In the UK, however, show equipment must be white in most competitions.)

LEFT: The domestic cat, as tame and docile as it has become, remains a carnivore at heart, and must have meat or fish to lead a healthy life.

Cats are taken to the judge's table one at a time. For this part of the judging, you should get your cat used to being held up at arm's length as a judge would when examining it. Place one hand under the front legs, and scoop it up by pushing your other hand under its hind quarters. Bring the cat up level with your chest, supporting its full weight underneath and leaning the cat against you. A kitten is small enough to sit on your palm as long as you have your other hand around its neck to support the head.

For each pedigree breed there is a standard of points against which the cat is evaluated. For non-pedigree cats, there is no scale of points, so the cat is judged on condition, grooming, colouring, attractive features and temperament when handled. Once the judge has examined every cat in a class, the judge personally places the rosettes on the pens in the winning order, and the results are then announced. After the various judges have nominated their five best cats and five best neuters, a top

FAULTS WHEN SHOWING CATS

THE following traits are faults in any breed under GCCF rules. For show regulations in other countries, check with your local cat fancy.

- Tail faults, such as kinks

- White hairs or patches in any breed other than whites or tortie and whites

- Polydactylism (extra toes)

- Monorchidism or Cryptorchidism (missing testicles)

- Uneven jaw lines

- Misaligned bites

- Any cat that has been declawed will be refused entry to a show

TO FIND OUT THE MOST COMMON FAULTS FOR EACH BREED, SEE THE SPECIFIC ENTRY FOR THAT BREED IN THE SECOND PART OF THIS BOOK.

judge assesses all these cats until the five best in each section have been chosen. Eventually, an overall 'Best Cat' is chosen.

LEFT: The luxurious coat of the Persian is known as a double coat because it has both a soft, woolly undercoat and a longer, coarser, outer coat of guard hairs.

BELOW: Every detail of a cat, such as long or short hair, is determined by the genetic code contained in its 19 pairs of chromosomes.

ABOVE: **M**utations, while
infrequent, do occur regularly
enough to give rise occasionally
to new breeds, such as the
Scottish Fold.

BECOMING A
BREEDER

There are two ways to enter the world of cat fancy. The easiest and least involved is to purchase a pedigree kitten or cat from an established breeder and begin entering it in shows. The more difficult and perhaps more rewarding is to obtain one or two female kittens. Don't buy an entire male (stud), but be sure that you can find a suitable tom for stud. Females reach sexual maturity between seven and 12 months, males between 10 and 14. Most breeds should give litters only once a year, but Oriental types can give birth every seven or eight months without ill effects.

To increase your chances of producing kittens with excellent showing prospects,

ABOVE: **M**ost breeds of cat should be allowed to produce a litter no more than once a year, although the oriental types can give birth every seven or eight months without ill effects.

choose a champion stud with features that compensate for any weaknesses in your queen. For example, if her eyes are too small for her type, choose a stud with eyes of the correct size. Check out studs carefully, making sure they have veterinary and pedigree certificates. You will have to pay for the stud's services, but if the first mating proves unproductive, a second mating may be provided free of charge.

All the characteristics of a particular breed are passed on from parent to offspring in the genes, which are situated on the chromosomes. The domestic cat has 38 chromosomes, in 19 pairs (humans have 46, in 23 pairs). Each chromosome contains a 'blueprint' for every detail of the animal.

Concepts of selective breeding were first discovered in the mid-nineteenth century by an Austrian monk named Johann Gregor Mendel. Using peas, Mendel learned that certain patterns of inheritance can be anticipated. Mendel's first 'law' states that if two parents differ in only one trait, for which one has dominant genes and the other has two recessive genes, all the offspring of the first generation will display the dominant gene trait. For example, because black is dominant over blue, a true-breeding black-coated parent and a true-breeding blue-coated parent will have black-coated kittens.

The second 'law' states that crossing of the offspring of the original pair will then produce variety in that very trait. Some will look like each of the grandparents in that trait, and some will look completely different. Some of the next generation will have black coats, some will have blue coats, and some will have other coats. Breeders commonly use inbreeding (breeding offspring) to create the 'ideal' cat. Caution, however, must be exercised because, in addition to promulgating the best characteristics of a breed, inbreeding can bring out mutant traits, good and bad.

Mutation has led to the beginning of breeds such as the Sphynx, American Wirehair, Cornish Rex and Devon Rex. Mutant genes tend to give rise to new colour varieties rather than entirely new breeds, which is how breeders developed a dozen varieties of Burmese. Mutation may also explain how kittens of domestic cats are born domestic. With most wild species, the domestication process must be repeated with each new generation.

Even some normal genes can produce negative effects. For example, the dominant white gene can induce deterioration of the inner ear, causing deafness in white cats, especially those with blue eyes. The Siamese gene can cause reduced binocular vision and double vision.

MATING AND REPRODUCTION

To become pregnant, your queen needs to be in oestrus (heat). Just before that period, she will be unusually affectionate and involve herself in more rubbing, rolling and licking than usual. When she enters oestrus, she will exhibit restlessness and anxiety to seek out a mate, howling and calling.

Feline heat cycles are seasonal in most breeds and tend to start in December or January until the following September. Most kittens arrive in July and August. Oestrus normally lasts about three weeks, but is only very noticeable for one week. When it begins, arrange for the queen and stud to spend time together. Relevant pedigree and health certificates should accompany the cats, and health checks may be required before the meeting begins. The two should be placed in adjacent quarters, separated by a door or mesh. When the queen begins to make advances, she should be allowed into his quarters. Either before or after mating, the queen may strike out at the tom, scratching, clawing and spitting. To protect himself, the male must have ample space to retreat during these periods.

Ejaculation occurs as soon as the tom enters the queen. Then they separate, and the tom distances himself from her. They should be permitted to mate several times over three or four days. It is most important to keep the queen in for a week after she has been to stud as she may still be calling and be mated by local tom-cats. Dual conceptions are then possible; kittens born from dual conceptions cannot be registered with the GCCF.

The queen may not show signs of being pregnant until approximately two weeks after mating. If she is pregnant, her nipples will redden (pink-up), she will gain 1-2 kg (2-4 lb), her abdomen will swell, and she will become restless.

Pregnancy itself lasts about nine weeks (65 days). Kittens born earlier than 58 days tend to be delivered dead or weak and should be regarded as miscarriages. Those born later than 71 days are likely to be bigger than normal, and may be dead. Most queens have no trouble giving birth, but it's a good idea to keep the cat under veterinary care in case problems arise. Also make sure your queen eats a nutritious diet during her pregnancy, up to three or four meals a day if she desires.

Before the kittens arrive, provide the queen with a choice of nesting sites. Cardboard boxes lined with paper towels are suitable because they can be changed easily and will not smother the kittens. The mother-to-be should be confined to the room with the chosen box once she starts having contractions.

The first stage of labour – contractions – may last up to six hours. During this

ABOVE: **M**ost kittens are born in July and August, but this varies with the exact heat cycle of each individual female.

BELOW: Nearly all kittens are born with blue eyes, which change to other colours as they mature.

time, the queen will be quite anxious and restless. She may also have a vaginal discharge, clear or cloudy water and some blood. Soon, she will bear down, and the first kitten will emerge as a protrusion from the vagina. Once the kitten is born, the queen will free it from the membranes, bite off the umbilical cord, and lick each kitten to encourage it to breathe. Try to discourage the mother from eating the afterbirth.

Each kitten will be born separately, with its own membranes and placenta. The time between each kitten can be as little as a few minutes or as long as several hours. Most litters consist of four or five kittens. To determine which are male or

RIGHT: Litters generally consist of four or five kittens, although some breeds average more and others fewer. Feral cats often produce the largest litters, probably in response to their uncertain environment.

female at this early stage, note that females generally have less space between the anal hole and the genitals than males. When all the kittens are born, the mother will clean them while they feed. Make sure each kitten finds a teat; each kitten will probably claim that particular teat as its own.

Keep the mother away from tom cats until after the kittens have been weaned because she may come into oestrus within a few days of giving birth and conceive again. A series of close-together pregnancies is likely to damage her health.

At birth, the kittens should be approximately 13 cm (5 in) long and weigh between 60 and 140 g (2-5 oz). Because they are

born with eyes closed and ears folded, they cannot see or hear. Therefore, their senses of smell and touch are vital in satisfying their needs for food and warmth. Although breeds differ, cats are approximately the equivalent of two to three human years old at three months of age, and reach about 18 in human years at the end of their first year. Then they age gradually, several equivalent human years every year, and are approximately 25 after two years, 30 after three years, 40 after five years, 50 after eight years and 60 after 10 years.

While they are still kittens, the mother communicates vocally at first, using various noises for scolding, greeting, enticing and warning. Later on, visual signals also become important. For example, the mother uses her tail to lead them. During their first few days, the mother may move the kittens to a new nest, to 'protect' them from predators. She may pick them up by the scruff of their necks with her mouth, but don't try this yourself as you do not have the necessary instincts to do it correctly. Queens also lick their kittens frequently, particularly their rear ends, stimulating them to relieve themselves. Kittens may instinctively hiss or spit if disturbed, even before their eyes open. Another protective habit is to bed down with their siblings, both for warmth and to keep the litter together.

The kittens' eyes begin to open in 5-10 days, and should be fully open by about 20 days. They are usually blue, but may change to a different permanent colour by about 12 weeks. The youngsters will start to crawl by about 20 days, walk by 25 days, run by five weeks, eat solid food after three weeks and be fully weaned by eight weeks. This timing will vary between different breeds, and indeed between individual kittens. Litter training can be started during the third week, and the kittens will start to wash themselves, play and hunt soon after.

RIGHT: **A** *comfortable nest is important to the queen and her litter in the initial weeks following birth.*

BELOW: **E***xpect kittens to engage in a great deal of 'fighting' with one another and with almost anything else in the home that strikes their fancy.*

By about the fifth week, they should be registered as pedigrees with one of the cat fancy associations. The certificate validates cats as authentic members of a particular breed by listing from four to seven generations of forebears.

Veterinary care should begin in the ninth week, with initial vaccinations; another vaccination at 12 weeks, followed by spaying (female) or neutering (male) at 16 weeks and 36 weeks respectively.

Although kittens can leave the nest after six weeks, they will not be totally independent of the mother (or a substitute) for another five months. If kittens become separated from the mother before they are weaned, you can either find a foster mother (a new mother who may have a spare teat) or bottle-feed). If no foster mother is available, use special cat milk substitute powder with water. The milk must first be heated to blood temperature: 38°C (101°F). A bottle made for premature human babies is usually suitable, but if not, try an eye-dropper. Grasp the kitten gently around the neck and push the 'teat' into its mouth. Don't rush the procedure or you may frighten or gag the kitten. After feeding, stimulate it to relieve itself by wiping its anal area with cotton moistened in warm water and stroke its belly very gently with your fingers.

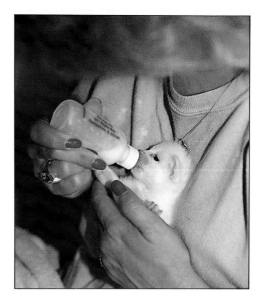

*LEFT: **K**ittens need their mother, or a substitute, for the first five or six months of their lives. Orphaned kittens can be raised on a bottle.*

Between feeds, keep kittens warm in a makeshift nest with disposable bedding, a heating pad or other harmless heat source, and some kind of mother-substitute such as a hot water bottle wrapped in a snuggly blanket. The nest temperature should be 25-30°C (77-86°F) during the first two weeks, and gradually reduced to 20°C (68°F) by the sixth week.

Start weaning the kittens at three weeks, introducing them to milky liquids at first, before adding a little cereal to their milk. A week later you can try them on a meat-based meal. Also include a multi-vitamin source in the daily diet. When the kittens first begin to eat solid foods, place them in the litter pan frequently, particularly when they crouch with their tails raised or have already begun to urinate or defecate. Never try to train them by rubbing their noses in their mistake if they use the wrong place. They will only be attracted by the scent and regard that area as a permanent 'toilet'.

Finally, don't be alarmed if your kittens appear to be absorbed in battle. These are only mock fights that teach them survival, hunting and social techniques. Be aware that they will probably also create mischief in places where you do not want them to be.

CHOOSING AND CARING FOR A CAT

Keeping a cat can be a costly exercise, in terms of food, cat litter and veterinary fees. And yet millions of people throughout the Western world enjoy the luxury of owning a cat. So if you do decide to become a cat owner, you will certainly not be alone. But before you jump in, take a little time to determine if your lifestyle is suited to cat ownership.

Do you have enough time to devote to care and companionship? Although cats do not require as much care as dogs, they still need daily love and attention. Do you have enough room for a cat's needs? Some cats are wanderers at heart, and also need exercise. If they lead a normal, active life, they will get all the exercise they need, exploring, chasing intruders, hunting and being curious. If you live in a flat or apartment or plan to keep your cat inside, choose a breed suited for these living conditions, not one known to prefer wandering. Breeds that do not take to an exclusive indoor life include Somali, Abyssinian and Rex. (See specific breed descriptions for further details). If you live in a congested area, you may want to exercise your cat on a leash. Breeds that will adapt better to a leash than others include Siamese, Burmese, Russian Blue, Colourpoint Shorthairs and Oriental Shorthairs.

Can you afford the food, dishes, collar, leash, licence (if applicable), inoculations, boosters, medical care, bed, toys, grooming tools and other cat paraphernalia? Although you won't need to provide constant entertainment for your cat, you will need to provide it with some basic essentials.

If you answer 'yes' to all these questions, then the next step is deciding which cat is for you. Do you want a pedigree or non-pedigree cat? If you want to try your hand at breeding, you'll need a pedigree. If not, other considerations are more important. Bear in mind too that a pedigree can involve considerably more financial outlay than an ordinary cat. (See the later section on breeds to determine which breed best suits your lifestyle and needs.)

Where should you obtain your cat? If you want a pedigree, check with local breeders. If not, go to someone who has

RIGHT: **C**ats are naturally clean animals, learning to groom themselves from an early age. Some grooming by the owner is also needed to keep the cat in top condition for showing.

kittens or the local animal shelter. It's best to stay away from pet shops, where animals sometimes pick up diseases and parasites.

Should you spay or neuter it? In the United States, animal shelters handle approximately 4.5 million felines a year; more than 60 per cent of these are destroyed. So if you are not planning to breed, avoid bringing more unwanted kittens into the world.

Will its claws bother you? Declawing disqualifies a cat from showing in the US and is illegal in the UK. Most experts believe it to be an unnecessary mutilation because claws are trimmed down naturally with exercise. If your cat does not spend much time outdoors, trim its claws regularly as an alternative to declawing. You can also help the natural process by providing a scratching post. Untrimmed claws may grow into the paw pad and cause health problems.

Male or female? Both sexes are affectionate and make good pets, but females in general are more affectionate. Unneutered males spray, wander and may fight; unneutered females have periods of heat and possibly unwanted pregnancies.

Kitten or adult? Kittens need more attention, so an older cat may be better if you plan to be absent during the day throughout the breaking-in period. Kittens are also more energetic, so think twice about acquiring one if your lifestyle would be upset because of that. Kittens, however, find it easier to settle in from the start because they are too young to remember their previous home.

Is the cat healthy? Before you finalize ownership, have a veterinarian check the animal's coat, eyes, nose, ears, mouth, teeth, abdomen and anal area for signs of disease or defects. If the cat passes its medical check, make and keep regular appointments for check-ups, vaccinations

RIGHT: **I**t is a good idea to accustom a cat to handling when it is still young. This is the best way to lift a cat, supporting the hindquarters with one hand.

and booster shots.

At the time when you acquire your new cat, make sure you have all the necessary equipment: litter box, litter, bed, collar, food dish, food, water bowl, grooming tools and scratching post. Place the food, water, litter and bed in a safe, draught-free place that you think the cat will like. Make sure your house is cat-proof, for the animal's sake as well as for the protection of your valuables and breakables. Take note of whether you have any toxic plants (*Caladium, Dieffenbachia, Euphorbia pulcherrima, Hedera, Nerium oleander, Philodendron, Prunus laurocerasus, Rhododendron, Solanum capiscastrum* and *Viscum*

TOP RIGHT: **M***any adult cats retain a playful attitude towards life, especially when kittens are available to enhance the atmosphere.*

CENTRE RIGHT: **A***s adorable as the kittens may be, millions of unwanted cats are born into the world each year. Spaying or neutering is often the humane choice for those cats that will not be bred intentionally.*

album), and the location of trash cans, stove, fireplace, cupboards, closets, balconies, electrical cords, ornaments and decorations. If you have other pets or young children, introduce the cat to its area and the other members of the household gradually, never unsupervised, until they are used to each other.

A cat's affinity has to be won. Unlike a dog, it won't remain with an inferior owner out of a misdirected sense of devotion. However, a cat will recognize a good owner and respond with affection and companionship. For best results, understand its nature and treat it not as a possession, but as a familiar guest.

A cat expresses affection by rubbing against peoples' legs, licking a hand or face, or lying on its back awaiting a caress and then immediately biting the hand that touches it. It often closes its eyes in sheer enjoyment of physical contact with its owner. Sometimes a cat will enact a 'ceremony' before settling down on its owner's lap or stretching out on a cushion: it will perform a 'pin dance', repeatedly pushing its claws into whatever it plans to rest on.

Your cat will need to learn to use the litter box, to come when called, and respond to other essential commands depending on your household. You may also be able to teach it to sit, beg, eat with its paws, walk on a leash, open a door, roll

BOTTOM RIGHT: **T***he offspring of top members of pedigree breeds, such as Himalayans, can be extremely expensive.*

FACING PAGE: **O***wners who have other smaller pets in the home must always be aware that the cat's natural instincts are to hunt and kill.*

RIGHT: Trimming a cat's claws is easily performed at home or by a veterinarian, making declawing an unnecessary mutilation.

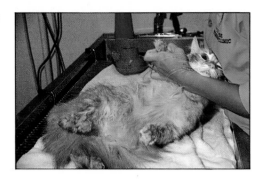

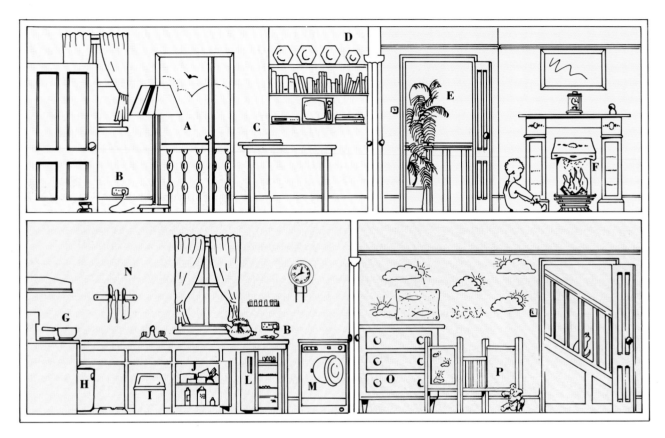

CREATING A 'CAT-SAFE' ENVIRONMENT

Cats are naturally curious, and good climbers; you will need to take some precautions to create a safe home for yourself and for your pet. Common dangers around the house are: (A) doors leading on to high balconies left open; (B) electrical cables which the cat might chew; (C) objects resting on table edges; (D) fragile objects on shelves; (E) poisonous houseplants; (F) fires without fireguards; (G) boiling pans which the cat might spill; (H) open oven doors; (I) accessible rubbish bins containing sharp objects; (J) household cleansers and detergents; (K) boiling kettles; (L) open refrigerators; (M) open washing machines or clothes dryers; (N) sharp utensils left out; (O) drawers left open; (P) babies or young children left alone in a room with a cat.

over, fetch objects and perform other tricks. You can also teach it not to do things, such as scratch furniture or lie on your bed, by scolding it with a 'shoo' or 'no'.

Cats may spend up to a third of their waking hours grooming themselves, using their barbed tongues, their forepaws and their teeth. Grooming is necessary to rid the cat's body of parasites and matted fur. It also has a nutritional function, providing vitamin D, produced on the fur by sunlight. In hot weather, saliva licked on to fur serves the same function as sweat, controlling body temperature by evaporation. That's why cats groom themselves more in warm weather and after play, hunting or other activity.

Mutual grooming is also normal in healthy cats, a behavioural trait carried over from the days when the mother groomed the kittens, sustaining the social bond. But excessive grooming should be

LEFT: **U**nlike dogs, cats will not continue to give their devotion to an uncaring, inferior owner. Their trust and affection must be won continuously.

BELOW LEFT: **A**s much as a third of a cat's waking hours are spent in the time-consuming task of grooming itself.

BELOW RIGHT: **C**ats are naturally drawn to plants, even though many household species of plant can be quite toxic. Plants must be one consideration among many in cat-proofing a home.

discouraged; it causes skin inflammation, hair loss and occurrence of fur balls in the digestive tract. Owners should also groom their cats regularly, if for no other reason than to provide an opportunity to check their condition and to get their cats used to it in case they ever need intensive grooming.

Although they have long been domesticated, cats still eat the typical meat-centred carnivorous diet. They need about 25-30 per cent protein and up to 40 per cent fat. Cats do not do well on vegetarian diets.

There are certain disorders and parasites to which cats are vulnerable. This is one reason why vaccinations are required

TOP LEFT: **D**omestic cats are hunters. This is a natural reflection of their ancestry, no matter how domesticated they may seem to be.

CENTRE LEFT: **W**ith proper care and attention, a cat can spend more than 15 years as an affectionate companion.

FACING PAGE: **C**ats need about 25-30 per cent protein in their diet. Although milk is a good source for kittens, meat and fish are better for adults.

BELOW: **B**athing is a regular necessity. Different cats will react to the experience differently. The initial introduction to the process plays a major role in determining future reactions.

at 8-12 weeks for feline distemper, upper respiratory problems and rabies. The vaccinations are not effective until about a week after the second dose, and annual boosters are required, usually at the annual check-up. Fleas, ticks, mites and maggots are some of the external parasites to be aware of.

Internal parasites include worms (round, hook, whip, thread, tape) and single-celled organisms. The single-celled protozoan *Toxoplasma gondaii* is especially harmful because it can spread to humans; pregnant women are advised to not handle soiled cat litter because the organism can cause miscarriage. Regular worming is advised for prevention of these problems.

Your cat's health could be in jeopardy if it vomits, collapses, bleeds, has dilated pupils, diarrhoea, or no appetite for more than one day. Check regularly for listlessness, cloudy eyes, closed eyelids, mouth odour, limping, pain when touched, constipation, frequent urination, and discharges. With proper care and love, a cat can live more than 15 years, providing years of affectionate companionship and possibly even prizes too.

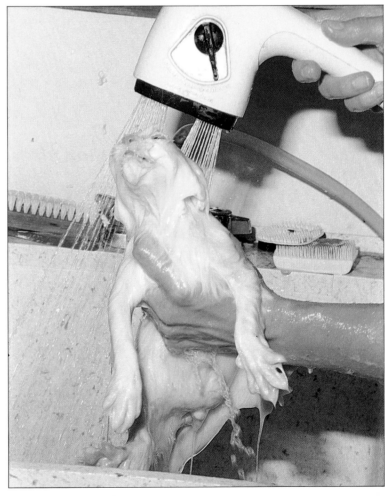

LEFT: **K**ittens require a great deal of attention, which they more than repay with their 'cute' and playful presence.

SHORTHAIR
BREEDS

ABYSSINIAN

Agouti Abyssinian

PLACE OF ORIGIN:	*Abyssinia*
COAT COLOUR:	*agouti, red, blue, cream*
COAT PATTERN/TYPE:	*ticked hairs*
EYE COLOUR:	*gold to green to hazel*
BUILD:	*medium, between oriental and cobby*
HEAD TYPE:	*modified oriental*

Blue Abyssinian

The mummified remains of some Ancient Egyptian cats are almost perfect copies of cats found in Abyssinia (today's Ethiopia) at the end of the nineteenth century. The Egyptian cats had 'ticked' (agouti) tawny hair, golden at the roots, and a similar-shaped head. There were also black and blue cats in Ancient Egypt. This led experts to believe that the Abyssinian (affectionately known as the 'Aby') and the Egyptian cat may have come from the same wild ancestor, the African Kaffir cat.

Others assert that the breed was established from tabby matings, a possibility because every now and then Abyssinian-type kittens are born to ordinary tabby parents. And even pedigree Abyssinians sometimes have kittens with tabby markings.

A male cat called Zulu, taken to Great Britain by soldiers returning from the Abyssinian War in 1868, became the basis for the British breeding programme. The breed was recognized in 1882 in Britain and by 1905 in the United States. These cats were initially known by other names besides Abyssinian, including Hare Cat, Rabbit Cat and Bunny Cat, because their coat is similar to that of the wild hare or rabbit. The coat is short, but has several bands of ticking.

Abyssinians come in a number of different colours. Agouti and red are the most common, but there are also blue and beige or cream varieties. Their eyes range from gold to green to hazel. In both Britain and the United States, the ideal 'Aby' is a medium-sized cat of modified oriental type, with a firm, muscular body. American standard calls for a slightly rounder head. Faults include signs of cobbiness, white marks on the neck, and random spots on the legs, neck and tail.

The 'Aby' came close to extinction during both World War I and World War II, when food scarcities struck everywhere in Europe. Meat, which is an essential need for all cats, but more so for the Abyssinian, was in extremely short supply. It had recovered, however, by the 1960s and '70s, only to suffer a severe setback with the outbreak of the feline leukemia virus.

Although it is rather rare, partly because it tends to bear small litters, the Abyssinian is a very popular cat, and is now enjoying another strong period of recovery.

AMERICAN SHORTHAIR
(Domestic Shorthair)

PLACE OF ORIGIN:	*United Kingdom (brought to North America in 1600s)*
COAT COLOUR:	*any except chocolate and lavender*
COAT PATTERN/TYPE:	*any except Himalayan*
EYE COLOUR:	*various*
BUILD:	*large, muscular*
HEAD TYPE:	*oblong with large ears*

Silver Tabby American Shorthair

Black American Shorthair

Although known today as a very common cat, the American Shorthair probably came to America with the blue-blooded humans who set sail on the *Mayflower* in the 1600s.

In Britain, American Shorthairs were bred from the same stock as the British Shorthair, which was developed from cats taken to Britain by the Romans. Belle, a male pedigree red tabby, sent from England to a cat lover in America, was the first shorthair to be registered officially as a pedigree by the Cat Fanciers' Association (CFA). So the first registered American Shorthair was actually a British Shorthair. The first home-bred American Shorthair, named Buster Brown, was registered in 1904. This male smoke of unknown American parents opened the way for the American stock, called Domestic Shorthair until 1966. By the late 1950s, the CFA stud book listed 50 Domestic Shorthairs.

Non-pedigree cats are still called domestics, and until January 1985, were accepted by the CFA as foundation stock. To strengthen its roots as a natural American breed, associations began to allow registration of non-pedigree cats. In 1971 one of these was honoured as the 'Best American Shorthair of the Year' by the CFA. Almost any colour and coat combination are permitted for this breed, except chocolate and lavender, and Himalayan patterns are not allowed. Varieties include white, black, blue, red, cream, bicolour, shaded silver, chinchilla, tortoiseshell, calico and tabby. Males generally weigh about 6.5 kg (14 lb), and females 4.5 kg (10 lb). They have muscular bodies with well-developed shoulders and chests. Their legs are firm and strong, and they have oblong, rather than round, heads and large ears. Their eyes, set well apart, come in a variety of colours. Faults common in this breed include thinness or heaviness, too long or lightweight hair, short tail and random white spots.

American Shorthairs are tough and hardy, having survived the new life and climate when their ancestors were moved from Britain to the New World. They are intelligent, affectionate, home-loving and like children. They are still regarded as working cats, for they have continued to be good 'mousers', and enjoy being outdoors and on the farm.

AMERICAN WIREHAIR

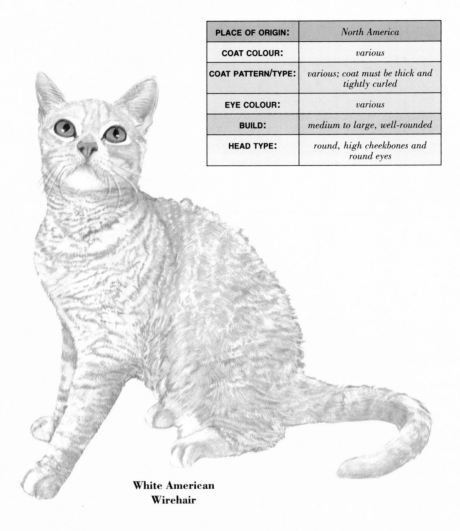

PLACE OF ORIGIN:	*North America*
COAT COLOUR:	*various*
COAT PATTERN/TYPE:	*various; coat must be thick and tightly curled*
EYE COLOUR:	*various*
BUILD:	*medium to large, well-rounded*
HEAD TYPE:	*round, high cheekbones and round eyes*

White American Wirehair

The American Wirehair is a good example of spontaneous mutation. It happened in 1966 in Verona, New York State, to Adam, a red and white American Shorthair. Instead of the usual American Shorthair coat, he was born with a curly, wiry coat that bore more resemblance to a lamb's fleece.

Adam was taken by a breeder and mated with one of his littermates, a brown tabby tortoiseshell (torbie). Of their four kittens, two were red and white wirehairs. One of them, Amy, later gave birth to other wirehaired kittens. Among them was Barberry Ellen, the first true-breeding American Wirehair.

Both Adam and Amy were too long and slim for the American Shorthair standard, so breeders attempted to improve the body while retaining and thickening the wiry coat. Because the wirehaired gene is dominant, it was poss-ible to outcross for these improvements without losing the coat trait.

The use of longhaired breeds for mating was avoided to maintain the distinct coat appearance. The ideal coat must not be patchy, although on underparts it should be less wiry. It should be of medium length, tightly curled, thick, coarse, resilient and springy. Faults are long or soft coat, and colours that might induce hybridization.

American Wirehairs have been bred in a variety of colours, and in 1977 were given championship status by the CFA. The name American Wirehair comes from the canine Wirehaired Terrier because the coats are so similar.

The American Wirehair resembles the American Shorthair in build and personality. It is affectionate and makes a good pet.

BOMBAY

PLACE OF ORIGIN:	North America
COAT COLOUR:	black
COAT PATTERN/TYPE:	solid colour: close-lying fur
EYE COLOUR:	gold or copper
BUILD:	lithe and muscular
HEAD TYPE:	broad with rounded ears

Brilliant gold or copper eyes accentuate the lustrous black coat of the Bombay. The fur is short and close-lying, giving the appearance of patent leather. Because of the contrast, some have called it 'the patent leather kid with the new penny eyes'.

Named after the city of Bombay because of its resemblance to the Indian black leopard, it is, nevertheless, an American breed. It was created by successful crossings between sable-brown Burmese and black American Shorthairs. The breeding programme began in 1958, but it was only in 1976 that the CFA accepted it for championship status.

The coat is its most charming feature. Acceptable eye colour ranges from gold to copper, but the darker coloration is preferred.

The body should be reminiscent of its Burmese ancestry – lithe and muscular. The head should be broad, the eyes well spaced, the ears rounded, the neck narrow. Faults include a kink in the tail, curly hair, spots, green eyes and colouring other than black.

This delightful cat is content in a flat or apartment and may never feel a need to go outside. But it also craves company so it shouldn't be left alone for too long. It is quiet, sensitive, affectionate, reserved, intelligent and soft-voiced. Its ears prick at the slightest sound, and it seems to have a particular dislike for loud noises.

Each litter has four to five light-coloured kittens, which become totally black by their sixth month.

BRITISH SHORTHAIRS

PLACE OF ORIGIN:	*United Kingdom*
COAT COLOUR:	*various (see main text)*
COAT PATTERN/TYPE:	*various; short, dense fur*
EYE COLOUR:	*various*
BUILD:	*sturdy on short legs*
HEAD TYPE:	*broad, rounded*

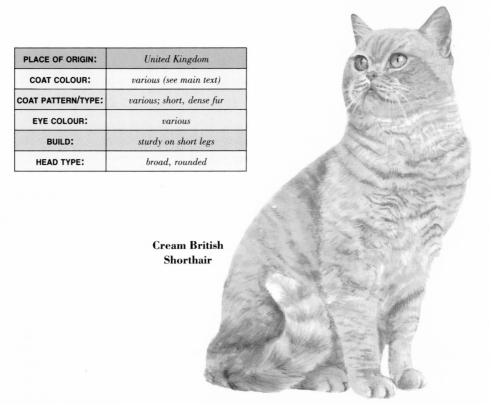

Cream British Shorthair

British Shorthairs are sturdy, healthy cats with strong, muscular bodies on short legs, and short, dense coats. They have broad, rounded heads with short, straight noses and large, round eyes. They come in a wide range of colours and patterns: from the solid-coloured black to the pure white, and from the discreetly tipped blue smoke to the bold-patterned silver tabby.

Today's British Shorthairs started with domestic cats taken to Britain by Caesar and the conquering Romans. (Their counterparts are the European Shorthair and the American Shorthair.) During the 400 years that the Romans ruled Britain, these housecats mated with the local European wildcats, but careful breeding since the nineteenth century has produced shorthaired cats that conform to a set standard.

Harrison Weir, who in 1889 wrote the first extensive book on cats, in which the British Shorthair was given the most prominent place, so loved the British street cat that he almost single-handedly elevated it to a registerable breed. Until the turn of the century, the British Shorthair was the most popular cat in the cat shows held at the Crystal Palace in London. Then the exotic Persians and Siamese captured the fancy. It was not until the 1930s that the

British Shorthair regained popularity.

They lost ground, as did all breeds, during World War II. After the war, there were so few pedigree Shorthair studs left that breeders, to perpetuate the breed, crossed British Shorthairs with Siamese and Persians, creating cats that were too lanky or woolly. Conscientious selective breeding programmes, however, finally brought the British Shorthair back to its desired square shape, with short, firm and thick fur.

Ideal British Shorthairs are short and sturdy, with legs short and strong, and tails short and thick, and rounded at the tip. Their heads are massive and rounded, with ears and eyes set wide over full cheeks. Their short, straight noses and firm chins rise from short, round necks.

Big, round eyes reveal an animal with inner strength that can handle almost any situation. Faults are long or puffy coats, nose stop and abnormal tail.

All British Shorthairs, of whatever colour or pattern, are quiet, gentle and affectionate pets. They are also known for being brave and able to take care of themselves. There are many stories of British Shorthairs who warned their owners of impending danger, and of mother cats who fiercely defended their young.

BRITISH TABBY SHORTHAIR

**Silver Spotted British
Tabby Shorthair**

PLACE OF ORIGIN:	*United Kingdom*
COAT COLOUR:	*various (see main text)*
COAT PATTERN/TYPE:	*various; short, dense fur*
EYE COLOUR:	*various*
BUILD:	*sturdy on short legs*
HEAD TYPE:	*broad, rounded*

**Brown British Tabby
Shorthair**

The British Tabby Shorthair comes in three coat patterns: classic, mackerel and spotted. All three models exist in a variety of colours: silver, brown, red, brown, cream and blue.

The word 'tabby' is said to come from a type of ribbed skin or taffeta that was developed in an area of old Baghdad known as Attabiya. It is believed that all domestic cats once had tabby markings and, if all those alive were allowed to mate freely, eventually only tabby cats would survive.

All three tabby types, classic, mackerel and spotted, have the letter 'M' marking on their forehead, said to stand for the prophet Muhammad, from when he embraced the cat. The classic tabby pattern is also called marbled or blotched. It includes 'necklaces', 'bracelets' and 'rings' on the tail. A line runs unbroken from the corner of each eye, with three stripes running down along the spinal column.

The mackerel tabby looks more like a tiger, even though it is named after a fish. It has a series of narrow lines running vertically down the spine, and fine lines running outwards from the eyes towards the shoulders. The lips and chin should be the same colour as the rings on the eyes. The back of the back paw should be black, the nose should be red, and the eyes either orange or copper.

The spotted tabby goes back to Ancient Egypt. The spotted effect is caused by breaks in the classic tabby lines. The spots should be distinct and numerous, forming round, oval or rosette shapes.

A line runs from the corner of each eye to behind the head, and a stripe runs down the spine. There should be a double row of spots on the underside.

BRITISH SPOTTED SHORTHAIR

PLACE OF ORIGIN:	*United Kingdom*
COAT COLOUR:	*various (see main text)*
COAT PATTERN/TYPE:	*various; short, dense fur*
EYE COLOUR:	*various*
BUILD:	*sturdy on short legs*
HEAD TYPE:	*broad, rounded*

**Red British Spotted
Shorthair**

This is the breed portrayed in Egyptian mythology as the killer of an evil serpent. Known as 'Spottie', the British Spotted Shorthair has a coat very similar to the mackerel tabby, only broken into spots. It can be created in any tabby colour, with red, brown and silver being the favourites. Red is light, spotted in deeper red, with deep orange or copper eyes. Brown is pale with black spots and copper or gold eyes. Silver is pale grey, spotted with black, and highlighted by greenish eyes. There should not be any white.

The Spottie, exhibited at the first shows in the nineteenth century, is affectionate, friendly and intelligent.

BRITISH TORTOISESHELL SHORTHAIR

PLACE OF ORIGIN:	*United Kingdom*
COAT COLOUR:	*various (see main text)*
COAT PATTERN/TYPE:	*various; short, dense fur*
EYE COLOUR:	*various*
BUILD:	*sturdy on short legs*
HEAD TYPE:	*broad, rounded*

British Tortoiseshell Shorthairs (affectionately called 'Torties') are most often female because sex and colour are genetically linked. The few males that are born are genetically infertile. In the United States, tortoiseshell and white cats (as well as the British White Shorthairs) are also called calico.

The coat should be black and vibrantly patched with red and cream, and may have a red or cream blaze on the head. There should be some white on the paws, but always more coloured patches. Nose leather and pads should be pink, black or both. Eyes should be copper or orange. When shows began in the late nineteenth century, the Tortie was among the first to be exhibited. It is even-tempered, intelligent and affectionate.

BRITISH BICOLOUR SHORTHAIR

PLACE OF ORIGIN:	*United Kingdom*
COAT COLOUR:	*various (see main text)*
COAT PATTERN/TYPE:	*various; short, dense fur*
EYE COLOUR:	*various*
BUILD:	*sturdy on short legs*
HEAD TYPE:	*broad, rounded*

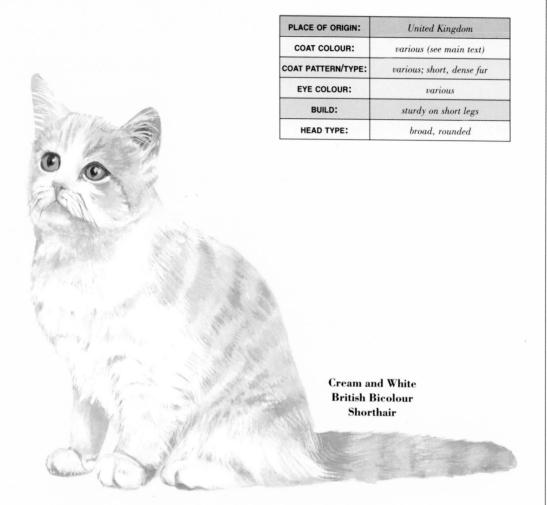

**Cream and White
British Bicolour
Shorthair**

The British Bicolour Shorthair has even patches of red, blue, black or cream on a white background. The underside, muzzle and feet should be white, and patches should show no tabby marks. Colour should be present on the face. Nose and paws should be pink or match the dominant patch colour. Eyes are always orange or copper, without green on the rims.

This breed was displayed in the 'other variety' classes until 1966, when it was given a breed number and championship status. The original standard, which required it to be marked like a Dutch rabbit (the mask being symmetrically split down the middle by colour), proved too difficult to replicate. Consequently, the standard was amended to demand only clear and even patches, with up to two-thirds coloured and a third white. Popular varieties in recent years are spotted, shaded and tipped.

BRITISH SMOKE SHORTHAIR

PLACE OF ORIGIN:	*United Kingdom*
COAT COLOUR:	*various (see main text)*
COAT PATTERN/TYPE:	*various; short, dense fur*
EYE COLOUR:	*various*
BUILD:	*sturdy on short legs*
HEAD TYPE:	*broad, rounded*

Black British Smoke Shorthair

This breed has a very unusual coat: a single-colour topcoat over a white undercoat. The topcoat is either black or blue. There should be no tabby or white markings. When the cat moves, a shimmering effect is produced by the layered colours.

This breed was developed in the late nineteenth century by crossing silver tabby and solid British Shorthairs.

Good-natured, affectionate and smart, it has orange or yellow eyes.

BRITISH TIPPED SHORTHAIR

PLACE OF ORIGIN:	*United Kingdom*
COAT COLOUR:	*various (see main text)*
COAT PATTERN/TYPE:	*various; short, dense fur*
EYE COLOUR:	*various*
BUILD:	*sturdy on short legs*
HEAD TYPE:	*broad, rounded*

**Cream British Tipped
Shorthair**

The British Tipped Shorthair is the short-haired version of the longhaired Chinchilla or Cameo Persian.

Ideally, it should have a white undercoat tipped with fur on the back, flanks, head, ears and tail in any of the recognized solid colours: black, blue, red, cream, chocoloate and lilac. There may be some vestigial tail rings, but no other tabby markings should be present. The chin, chest and stomach should be white.

Eye colours should be copper or orange, rimmed in rose, or in the black variety, green with black rims. Nose leather and paw pads should be pink or match the tipping. This type was created from mixes of silver, smoke and blue genes.

BURMESE

PLACE OF ORIGIN:	*Burma*
COAT COLOUR:	*brown only in US; also red, cream, blue, lilac, chocolate and tortoiseshell varieties in UK*
COAT PATTERN/TYPE:	*solid colour*
EYE COLOUR:	*yellow or gold*
BUILD:	*medium-sized, long body*
HEAD TYPE:	*rounded on top between wide-set ears*

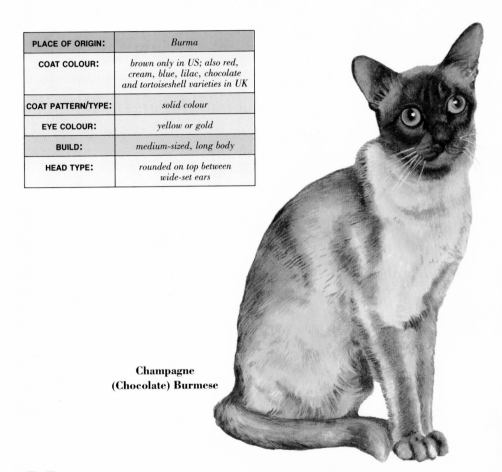

Champagne (Chocolate) Burmese

Nearly all modern pedigree Burmese cats can be traced back to one walnut-brown female, Wong Mau. She was taken from Rangoon to San Francisco in 1930 by Dr Joseph Thompson, a US Navy psychiatrist.

Thompson started the first pedigree breed to be developed completely in the United States. Because there were no similar cats with which to mate Wong Mau, Thompson arranged a mating with her closest cousin, a Siamese. Then he crossed the offspring and Wong Mau. All Wong Mau's kittens were hybrids. When mated back to her, brown kittens resembling their mother were the result. Thus began the Burmese line.

During the 1930s and early '40s, to reduce inbreeding, breeders imported several more Burmese cats from Burma. There were also some outcrossings to Siamese. The Burmese was first officially recognized by the CFA in 1936 and by the Governing Council of the Cat Fancy (GCCF) in 1952. But because the outcrossings with Siamese created too strong a Siamese look, the CFA suspended registration during the 1940s and '50s. The breed is now well established in Europe, Australia and New Zealand.

Burmese cats have coats like polished mahogany in the United States, but British standard recognizes them in many other colours: red, cream, blue, lilac, chocolate and tortoiseshell (various). All types have yellow or gold eyes which are slanted at the top and rounded at the bottom. They are medium-sized, long, graceful and muscular cats, with long necks, round chests, slender legs and slightly tapering tails. Their heads are rounded on top between their wide-set ears. The muzzle is shorter than that of the Siamese, with a strong chin and jaw.

Faults commonly found in Burmese cats include white marks under the throat, lines or bars on the coat, green or grey eyes, and too-dark a coloration.

All Burmese have happy dispositions and make excellent companions. Burmese generally live longer than other breeds, surviving into their middle teens.

COLOURPOINT SHORTHAIR

PLACE OF ORIGIN:	*Thailand*
COAT COLOUR:	*red-point, tabby-point, tortie-point (see main entry for details)*
COAT PATTERN/TYPE:	*points as for Siamese*
EYE COLOUR:	*clear blue*
BUILD:	*medium size, lanky, long legs*
HEAD TYPE:	*long and triangular*

Red Point Colourpoint Shorthair

Lilac Tortie Point Colourpoint Shorthair

The first Siamese had fawn-colour coats and seal-brown points on their ears, face, mask, legs, feet and tail. Later it was mixed with chocolate, lilac and blue points, which were accepted in the breed in the United States.

Many believe that these are the only true Siamese. When they were crossed with Abyssinians and other shorthairs to achieve more colours for points, the American organizations felt that they should be classed separately because of their non-Siamese genes. Thus was created the Colourpoint Shorthair.

In Britain, the GCCF calls them red points, tabby points (in varying hues) and tortie points (also in several colours).

Many new colours and patterns have been developed recently within the Siamese range. A British seal-point Siamese was mated in 1960 with a tabby to produce a single tabby among the seal-points. When the tabby was mated back to a seal-point, four of the kittens had tabby points. This new breed was recognized by the GCCF and the CFA several years later, and was called tabby-point Siamese in Britain and lynx-point in America.

Besides the four basic point colours, the Colourpoint is bred in red-point, red tabby-point, cream-point, cream tabby-point, seal tortie-point, seal tabby-point, chocolate tortie-point, chocolate tabby-point, lilac cream-point, lilac tabby-point, torbie-point, blue tabby-point and blue-cream point.

A new variety of Colourpoint Shorthair is the silver, called silver tabby-point and silver-blue tabby point. A silver tabby-point Siamese, still relatively rare, has a paler body coat than do other Siamese and is silver between the tabby stripes.

The coat of the Colourpoint Shorthairs is close, fine and shiny. All the other characteristics of the Colourpoint Shorthair are the same as the Siamese.

EGYPTIAN MAU

One of the more prominently patterned breeds, the Egyptian Mau, can have a spotted coat reminiscent of the leopard or a lined coat similar to that of the tiger. As might be expected, these imprints are very critical under the CFA standard. The forehead should display the classic 'M' pattern, with frown marks extending back and into spots on the spine.

In the 1950s, Princess Troubetskoy obtained a pair of Maus named Gepa and Ludol, which had originated in Egypt. It was not until some years later, in 1968 by the Cat Fanciers' Federation (CFF) and in 1977 by the CFA, that Americans finally gave recognition to the breed.

The type of these cats resembles that of the Abyssinian. It is a blend between the oriental

Bronze Egyptian Mau

PLACE OF ORIGIN:	*Egypt*
COAT COLOUR:	*bronze, silver, smoke*
COAT PATTERN/TYPE:	*spotted markings, barring on legs*
EYE COLOUR:	*light green*
BUILD:	*between oriental and cobby*
HEAD TYPE:	*slightly rounded with large ears*

Two 'mascara' lines around each of the eyes extend to the sides of the face. There is barring on the legs, with distinct matching spots being preferred on the body itself. On the underparts, spotting should contrast against the lighter coat colour.

Three body colours are permitted, and all are shown in the same class. The bronze has a bronze background with a creamy underside and brown patterning. The silver has a similar distribution of colour, set against charcoal-black markings. In the case of the smoke, the charcoal body has black patterning.

All colours have brown or black paw pads, and light green, almond-shaped eyes. The smoke has a black nose, while both silver and bronze have brick-red nose leathers. A natural breed, the Egyptian Mau originates from Cairo where it is said to be descended from the cats which were worshipped in Ancient Egypt. Another theory is that it was just bred to look like that ancient cat.

of the Siamese and the cobby of the longhair. They are active, muscular cats, of medium size with long legs. The head is slightly rounded with large, moderately pointed ears. Although they can be affectionate, they do not take naturally to strangers. Faults include blended or no spots, a small head, pointed muzzle, too-slanted eyes and the wrong eye colour.

The Egyptian Mau was imported to Britain for the first time in 1978. Prior to that, its description was used for another breed, now called the Oriental Spotted Tabby. There is a clear difference in body type between these two breeds. The Spotted Tabby has a more foreign appearance, probably from Siamese crossings. Its head markings are more pronounced, and it boasts a wider range of colours: blue, chocolate and lilac (where the eyes should be green); and red and cream (where eye colour can range from copper to vivid green).

53

EUROPEAN SHORTHAIR

PLACE OF ORIGIN:	*Africa/northern Europe*
COAT COLOUR:	*variety of colours regarded as distinct breeds*
COAT PATTERN/TYPE:	*various; fine, short fur*
EYE COLOUR:	*to match coat*
BUILD:	*solid, muscular*
HEAD TYPE:	*round with rounded ears*

Red European Shorthair

All good-quality shorthaired housecats of Europe are grouped together under the name 'European'. Although their exact origin is unknown, they probably descended from the African wildcat, and were introduced to northern Europe by the Romans about 2,000 years ago. Because it has retained its ancestral traits without interference from breeders and geneticists, the European Shorthair is thought to be the most unadulterated of all the breeds.

Large eyes, coloured to match the coat, are featured on the round head with rounded ears. The body is solid and muscular with hardy legs, round feet and a broad chest. The coat is fine and short.

Recognizing the various genes needed to perfect them, the many colours that are permitted are regarded as distinct breeds: European Black, European White, European Albino, European Cream, European Red, European Grey, European Tabby, European Marbled, European Tortoiseshell, European Tortoiseshell with White, European Blue-Cream and European Bicolour.

European Shorthairs are intelligent, lively and inquisitive, with a natural instinct to hunt mice and other animals. Their personalities vary between breeding programmes, and they can be happy either in a small apartment or on a farm estate.

The female especially attaches herself to the entire family because she enjoys the company. If the females are not carefully monitored during periods of oestrus, however, they can reproduce more frequently and with larger litters than other breeds.

EXOTIC SHORTHAIR

PLACE OF ORIGIN:	*North America*
COAT COLOUR:	*as for American Shorthair and Persian (Longhair)*
COAT PATTERN/TYPE:	*as for American Shorthair and Persian (Longhair), dense, plush fur*
EYE COLOUR:	*to match coat*
BUILD:	*cobby*
HEAD TYPE:	*round head, short nose*

Tabby Exotic Shorthair

Tortoiseshell Exotic Shorthair

This cat was created by American breeders for cat fanciers partial to Persians, but who did not want the responsibility of a long, flowing coat. It was produced in the early 1960s by coupling Persians with American Shorthairs. Burmese and British Shorthairs were also used but this mix has not been allowed since 1968.

The Exotic Shorthair is the only hybrid cross recognized in the United States. To be registered, a cat must be the product of one Persian and one American Shorthair parent, two Exotic Shorthair parents, or one Persian and one Exotic Shorthair parent.

Originally, all American shorthaired cats (except foreign types such as the Abyssinian and Siamese) were considered to be in one class. They were then known as Domestic Shorthairs, but since have been renamed American Shorthairs. Show judges used to award prizes to those shorthairs with shorter noses and smaller ears, so breeders crossed more Domestics with Persians to produce cats with those characteristics. They became very popular, but Domestic Shorthair breeders who stuck to crossing Domestic Shorthairs with Domestic Shorthairs pushed for separate classes.

Thus the CFA adopted two classes and two standards for American shorthaired cats: one for American Shorthair and one for Exotic Shorthair. Show requirements for the Exotic Shorthair are the same as those for Persian, but the coat should be dense, plush and soft. It should be dense enough to stand out, and of medium length – slightly longer than other shorthairs, but not long enough to flow. All colours and patterns of the American Shorthair and Persian are allowed, including cream and brown tabbies. Faults are feathery hair on the ears or tail, tufting between the toes, a delicate head and a kinked tail.

Exotics are affectionate and calm like Persians, and playful like American Shorthairs. They are very much suited to an indoor life.

HAVANA

PLACE OF ORIGIN:	*United Kingdom*
COAT COLOUR:	*chestnut-brown*
COAT PATTERN/TYPE:	*short fur*
EYE COLOUR:	*green or yellow-green*
BUILD:	*Siamese type*
HEAD TYPE:	*As Siamese, but rounder muzzle and round-tipped ears*

The Havana's short brown coat is a rich, chestnut-brown colour, much like the cigar or that of the Havana rabbit, after which the cat is named. It is a variety of Britain's Foreign Shorthair. It bears more resemblance to the Brown Oriental Shorthair of the United States than the Havana Brown, which has a different build. The Havana has a Siamese-type build and green or yellow-green, almond-shaped eyes.

All-brown cats have been treasured for years. Their beauty was celebrated by ancient poets, and they were said to protect people from evil. They arrived early in the West, and were shown to the public in the late 1800s as the 'Swiss Mountain Cat'. In 1930 a solid brown feline appeared, called 'Brown Cat'.

The Havana is the result of a selective breeding programme in the 1950s. The aim was to establish a breed with the graceful build of the Siamese without its pointed coat. The first kitten fulfilling this criterion was from a seal-point Siamese and a short-haired black of seal-point Siamese ancestry.

The breed was first exhibited in 1953, but it was not accepted by the GCCF until 1956, when it was named the Chestnut Brown Foreign. This name has since been changed to Havana. Even so, some thought it too closely resembled the Burmese. Havanas were recognized by the CFA in 1959 as Havana Browns. In the United States, they are judged to the same standard as the Russian Blue, except for the obvious colour distinction.

The British version of the Havana is a Siamese type that looks like the American Oriental Self Brown. The physique of the American Havana Brown is closer to that of the Russian Blue: shorter head and longer fur, and semi-cobby, rather than muscular, body.

The Havana likes to sit on people's shoulders and enjoys human company as well as that of other cats. It makes a good housecat, but also appreciates some access to outdoors, such as a terrace or porch. This sleek beauty often investigates objects by touching with its paws, rather than using the usual feline technique of smelling.

The kittens may look like bats because of their large ears and pink noses. Faults are white hairs, hooked tail and spots.

JAPANESE BOBTAIL

**Black and White
Japanese Bobtail**

PLACE OF ORIGIN:	*China and Korea*
COAT COLOUR:	*any, except Siamese or Abyssinian agouti*
COAT PATTERN/TYPE:	*silky, medium-length fur*
EYE COLOUR:	*to harmonize with coat*
BUILD:	*medium-sized, lean; hind legs longer than front legs*
HEAD TYPE:	*high cheekbones, large ears, triangular head*

Red Japanese Bobtail

Japanese Bobtail cats are regarded as lucky, and artistic representations of these *mi-ke* (pronounced mee-kay, meaning three-furred) cats, with right paw raised, are symbols of good fortune.

The coat is a combination of red, black and white fur. The breed's other unusual feature is the short, multi-kinked tail held close to the body. The bobbed tail is about 10 cm (4 in) long and has thicker fur than the body, making for a pompom look. The tail's natural appearance is slightly deceptive, though, because when allowed to curl it looks much shorter than it actually is. Because of its similarity to a rabbit's tail, it is known as a bobtail.

High cheekbones and slanted eyes (that harmonize with coat colour) give Japanese Bobtails a distinctive Japanese look; they also have large ears and a triangular head. Their bodies are medium-sized, well-muscled and lean, with hind legs longer than their front legs, but angled so that their spines appear level when standing. Although the norm of the silky, medium-length coat is red, white and black, a variety of colours is acceptable, except the Siamese or Abyssinian agouti patterns. Faults common in this breed are heavy bodies, round heads and long or uncurved tails.

This cat was around long before it was first mentioned a thousand years ago in a manuscript written by a tutor to the Empress of Japan. Originally from China and Korea, it was a familiar figure in prints and paintings, and is shown on the front of the Gotokuji Temple in Tokyo. It is said that the first cats to arrive in Japan were black, followed by white and then orange – thus the three-coloured fur came to be.

An American cat lover living in Japan sent the first three Bobtails to the United States after World War II. Later, when she returned, she took 38 cats with her. Japanese interest in the breed grew only after American judges visiting a Japanese show in 1963 praised them. They were recognized by the CFA in 1978, but the breed is still rare in the United States, and is not yet recognized in Europe.

Bobtails make ideal family animals, for they are affectionate, intelligent and lively, and good mousers. They are readily adaptable to life both inside and outside. The kittens are very large at birth, especially their heads and feet.

Although similar to the Manx, Japanese Bobtails are not related to them. The Bobtail's tail is due to a recessive gene and breeds true. The Manx's tail, however, is a genetic defect.

KORAT

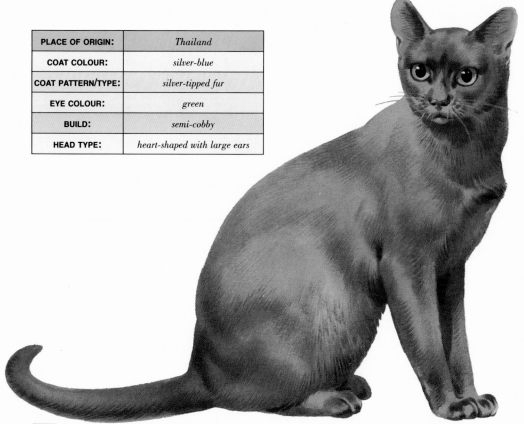

PLACE OF ORIGIN:	*Thailand*
COAT COLOUR:	*silver-blue*
COAT PATTERN/TYPE:	*silver-tipped fur*
EYE COLOUR:	*green*
BUILD:	*semi-cobby*
HEAD TYPE:	*heart-shaped with large ears*

The Korat (pronounced koh-raht) is one of the first cats mentioned in history. It comes from the province of Korat in Thailand (formerly Siam). There it is known as 'Si-Sawat', meaning good fortune, because its silver-blue fur resembles the seed of a fruit plant by that name.

Originally, Korats could be acquired only as a gift from an owner. It was also customary to give a Korat to royalty and other dignitaries as a sign of reverence. Even now, ownership of the Korat in Thailand is limited by the government. Today's Korat has the same features that typified its ancestors: heart-shaped face; large, curved ears; big, green, oval eyes; graceful, semi-cobby body; and silver-tipped coat.

The Korat probably first appeared officially at a National Cat Club Show in England in 1896. That blue cat entered in the Siamese class was disqualified for being 'blue instead of biscuit-colour'. The first registration in the United States was in 1959 of two Korats in Oregon – Nara and Darra. The Korat Cat Fanciers' Association was founded in 1965 to protect the purity of the breed and to ensure registration of cats only with Thai ancestry.

Korats were accepted for CFA championship status in 1966. By 1969 they were also recognized in Australia and South Africa. By 1975, they were accepted in Great Britain, but without championship status, because of opposition from fanciers who felt they were too similar to other recognized blue shorthairs.

Korats are gentle, intelligent and quiet. They love to be petted and enjoy the familiarity of their owners. Although good with children, they are guarded towards strangers and unwilling to accept strange cats. In fact, males can be aggressive and have a reputation as fighters in Thailand. That's why it's important to find a breeder who is selective about temperament, as well as physical traits.

This ancient breed sometimes displays a sense of duty to the family and has been known to alert them in a crisis. Korats are acutely aware of their surroundings and do not like to be startled by sudden noises. As a result, they may be nervous at shows.

Both kittens and adults are particularly susceptible to upper-respiratory viruses, so routine vaccinations are crucial. Both female and male care for kittens, which undergo an 'ugly duckling' stage and do not reach full radiance until they are about two years old.

MALAYAN

PLACE OF ORIGIN:	*North America (bred from Burmese)*
COAT COLOUR:	*champagne, blue and platinum*
COAT PATTERN/TYPE:	*solid colour*
EYE COLOUR:	*gold*
BUILD:	*medium sized, long bodies*
HEAD TYPE:	*rounded on top between wide-set ears*

Platinum Malayan

A recent breed, strictly American, the Malayan was officially recognized only in 1980. It is a twin of the Burmese, differing only in colour. Since they share the same genes, they also have the same inquisitive personality. They are athletic, affectionate, brave, sometimes bossy and very social.

In the United States only the sable-coloured cats are recognized by the CFA as true Burmese, while cats of three other colours are classified as Malayan: champagne, blue and platinum. In Great Britain and elsewhere, all cats of Burmese ancestry and form are labelled Burmese. There, colours other than sable are also recognized, namely red, cream and tortoiseshell (various).

The show standards for Malayans, as well as for American Burmese, differ from those in Britain, Europe, Australia and New Zealand. Americans prefer more rounded heads and eyes, whereas fanciers in other countries like wedge-shaped heads and more oval eyes. Malayans and Burmese in all countries have golden eyes.

Although Malayans are registered separately, they can be born spontaneously of Burmese parents. This is because they are descended from the same cat – Wong Mau. (See p.51 for an account of the Wong Mau line.) Faults commonly found in this breed include blue or green eyes, a kinky tail and white spots or streaks.

MANX

Black and White Manx

The Manx breed has two distinguishing features. The more obvious is its 'lack' of a tail. The second is that its hind legs are shorter than its front, leading to a rabbit-like walk.

Manx kittens are divided into four groups, depending on how little or how much tail they bear. The true exhibition Manx, known as a 'rumpy', has no tail at all, and may have a dimple instead. 'Rumpy-risers' have a few tail vertebrae, in the form of a little knob. 'Stumpies' have a short tail, maybe curved or

short back, which arches from the shoulders to the rounded rump, with the rump being considerably higher than the shoulders. The body will also have a plush double coat, with a cottony undercoat and a shiny overcoat. All colours are permitted, so there are solid, bicolour, tabby, calico, marbled and tortie coats. Breeders prefer to cross Manx with Manx, rather than with British or American Shorthairs, to be sure of getting the desired rounded look and double coat of fur. Faults are lack of undercoat, and a small head.

Brown Mackerel Tabby Manx

PLACE OF ORIGIN:	*Isle of Man, possibly earlier in Japan*
COAT COLOUR:	*all colours*
COAT PATTERN/TYPE:	*solid, bicolour, tabby, calico, marbled and tortie; plush double coat*
EYE COLOUR:	*to suit coat colour*
BUILD:	*rump higher than shoulders, short back*
HEAD TYPE:	*rounded head, medium-sized ears*

kinked, and usually movable. 'Longies' have a tail that is only slightly shorter than the norm.

All of the above may be registered as Manx cats, but only the rumpies may be exhibited – although rumpy-risers without a visible stump are allowed in a few associations. Even though they are barred from exhibiting, the last three categories are not shunned in breeding programmes. Actually, they are in much demand with breeders of Manx cats because an ongoing cross of two tailless Manx cats can eventually lead to fatal deformities of the vertebrae or the anus.

Both the British and American standards describe the Manx as rounded, especially in the rump, head and muzzle. The best Manx will have substantial cheeks, fat whisker pads, a slight nose dip, medium-sized ears with rounded tips, round eyes, a thick neck and a

There are several theories about the origin of the Manx. The most plausible is that in 1558, a ship from the Spanish Armada was wrecked off the Isle of Man coast. Tailless cats on board swam (yes, Manx do love water) ashore and began the Manx line. Whatever its origin, the original mutation must have occurred long ago, for the Manx breed was well established before the turn of the century. In 1901 a Manx Club was formed in Britain, and King Edward VII is said to have owned several Manx. Since its arrival in America in the 1930s, the Manx has been recognized by all American cat associations.

Throughout history the breed has had a band of faithful followers, who praise its intelligence, spirit, friendliness and hunting skills. The residents of the Isle of Man have even minted a coin with its image.

OCICAT

PLACE OF ORIGIN:	*North America*
COAT COLOUR:	*tawny, silver, blue, golden, chocolate sienna or lavender*
COAT PATTERN/TYPE:	*spotted tabby*
EYE COLOUR:	*copper, green, yellow, hazel or blue-green*
BUILD:	*medium to large*
HEAD TYPE:	*fine muzzle, large ears*

Silver Ocicat

Tonga, the first Ocicat kitten, reminded its breeder of a baby ocelot – hence the similar name 'Ocicat'. Because of its wild appearance yet gentle temperament, it has also been compared with Ancient Egyptian fishing cats, the Egyptian Mau and the Spotted Tabby Oriental.

The Ocicat is a hybrid, initially achieved by crossing a chocolate-point Siamese stud with a half-Siamese, half-Abyssinian queen. The offspring, spotted tabbies, were used to perpetuate the genetic inheritance. American Shorthairs have also been introduced into the programme, and breeders are working with these breeds – Siamese, Abyssinian and American Shorthair – to improve it. The Ocicat was accepted for registration by the Cat Fanciers' Association in the 1960s.

Females are medium size, and males are big, up to 7 kg (15 lb). Both are muscular, with well-proportioned heads, fine muzzles, large pricked ears and long, tapering tails. Mainly found in tawny (buff or ruddy) with black or brown spots, the polka-dotted form also comes in silver with black dots, blue with slate-blue dots, golden (bronze) with tarnished gold dots, golden with cinnamon dots (unique to Ocicats), chocolate with dull chocolate dots, sienna with beige or ecru dots, and lavender with darker lavender dots. Spots blending into the tabby pattern are a fault.

The eyes are copper, green, yellow, hazel or blue-green. Ocicats have dark lids, lined with a rim of the lightest colour of the coat. These cats love attention and respond well to people who enjoy having active, friendly animals.

ORIENTAL SHORTHAIR

PLACE OF ORIGIN:	*United Kingdom*
COAT COLOUR:	*solid, shaded, smoke, tabby and particolour*
COAT PATTERN/TYPE:	*short, fine fur*
EYE COLOUR:	*green or amber, green or blue in white Oriental Shorthair*
BUILD:	*as Siamese*
HEAD TYPE:	*as Siamese*

Shaded Cameo
Oriental Shorthair

Basically, the Oriental Shorthair is a solid-coloured Siamese. It was created in 1950, after a ruling by the Siamese Cat Club of Great Britain that only blue-eyed, pointed Siamese could be promoted as true Siamese. Some cat lovers then embarked on a post-war breeding programme to produce all-brown coated cats with the traditional 'foreign' body shape, mating Siamese for type with other shorthaired cats for colour. Thus was born the Havana (UK) or Brown Oriental Shorthair (US), followed soon after by other colours.

Each new colour is referred to as an individual breed in Britain and Europe, with names such as Foreign, Foreign Lilac etc. Collectively, they are known as Foreign Shorthairs. In the United States, all colours are called Oriental Shorthairs and judged as one breed. In American judging, this breed comprises 26 colours, divided into five groups: solids, shadeds, smokes, tabbies and particolours. A greater number of colours are accepted in Britain.

The Foreign White created by crossing Siamese with white Domestic Shorthairs, looks like a porcelain figurine, with sparkling white fur and shining blue eyes. While most blue-eyed white cats are deaf, the Foreign Whites seem to have escaped that fate. Although blue-eyed cats are preferred, green or gold eyes are permitted in the United States. Championship status was awarded to the Foreign White in 1977, and the breed had its first grand champion in 1979.

Except for blue eyes, the Oriental Shorthair show requirements are the same as those for the Siamese. In Britain, Foreign Whites must have blue, almond-shaped eyes; they must also be of medium size; have a long body; a wedge-shaped head and fine muzzle; large pointed ears; long, tapering tail; and possess a short, fine, tight, glossy coat.

The personality of the Oriental Shorthair is similar to the Siamese in that both demand a lot of attention.

REX
(Cornish and Devon)

PLACE OF ORIGIN:	*United Kingdom*
COAT COLOUR:	*as American and British Shorthairs*
COAT PATTERN/TYPE:	*curly fur with under and top coat (coarser in Devon Rex)*
EYE COLOUR:	*to suit coat colour*
BUILD:	*muscular with long legs*
HEAD TYPE:	*oriental type (more wedge-shaped in Devon Rex); curly eyebrows and whiskers*

**Blue Tabby
Devon Rex**

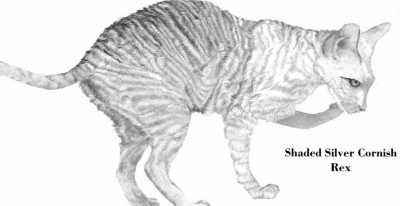

**Shaded Silver Cornish
Rex**

When a curly-coated cat named Kallibunker was born in 1950 to an otherwise normal litter in Cornwall, England, its owner, Nina Ennismore, got in touch with an expert cat breeder and rabbit fancier. On advice, she bred Kallibunker back to his mother, and more Rex kittens were produced. The recessive mutation was named after the similar mutation found in the rabbits. Two of Kallibunker's descendants, sent to America in 1957, founded the Cornish Rex line there.

In 1960, a curly-coated feral cat was observed living near Buckfastleigh in Devon, England. It was mated with a neighbour's young tortie-and-white stray to produce a kitten with curly fur, which was named Kirlee. When Kirlee and Kallibunker were mated, only straight-haired kittens resulted, making it obvious that both lines were mutations and would have to be advanced separately. It was also decided to breed towards two specific body types.

Three German Rexes were sent to the United States in the early 1960s, and when crossed with Cornish cats, curly kittens were created. The two distinct breeds – Cornish and Devon – were recognized for championship competition in 1967 in Britain. In the United States, the CFA established the Cornish Rex as distinct from the Devon Rex in 1979.

The GCCF standard for the Cornish Rex says that the breed should have a hard, muscular body with long, straight legs. The oriental-type head should have a straight profile, oval eyes, large ears and curly eyebrows and whiskers. The Devon Rex should have both under and top coat, but coarser hair than the Cornish. It should have a more wedge-shaped head with a pixie face.

Because they rarely shed and have fine fur, Rex make ideal pets for people allergic to cats. For those same reasons, they must be protected from extreme heat and cold. Their normal body temperature is a degree higher than other breeds, making them warm to the touch. This also gives them a higher metabolism and a correspondingly larger appetite.

Both Rexes are accepted in practically all colours of American and British Shorthairs. Si-Rex is a name for Rex with Siamese points. They are very inquisitive, affectionate, independent and talkative. Faults are chocolate hybridization, resemblance to oriental colours and kinked tails.

RUSSIAN BLUE

PLACE OF ORIGIN:	*Russia*
COAT COLOUR:	*bright blue*
COAT PATTERN/TYPE:	*short, silky fur*
EYE COLOUR:	*green*
BUILD:	*medium oriental type*
HEAD TYPE:	*wedge-shaped, large ears*

A unique feature of the Russian Blue is its short, plush, silky coat in a bright, even blue colour, with silver-tipped guard hairs. For contrast, it has striking green, almond-shaped eyes that slant towards the nose, and mauve nose leather and paw pads.

The Russian Blue is a medium oriental-type, leggy, with a long, slim neck and tail, and a graceful body. Its wedge-shaped head bears substantial whisker pads, large ears and a strong chin.

Common faults are obesity, wide head, spots, patterns and white hairs. They are tranquil, affectionate and intelligent cats. Because they like calm surroundings, they prefer families without rambunctious children and unnecessary noise. They are also loving towards each other and make good parents. Although they prefer an indoor life and love to sit by the fire, they can also withstand the cold, as did their Russian ancestors.

The Russian Blue is said to have been introduced to Europe in the 1860s by British sailors visiting the port of Archangel on Russia's northern seaboard. They have also been known as 'Archangel Blues', 'Maltese Blues', 'Spanish Blues', 'Chartreuse Blues', 'British Blues' and even 'American Blues'. They finally acquired their current name in the 1940s because similar cats originated in Russia.

It was shown in Great Britain around the turn of the century when all shorthaired blue cats competed in one class, whatever their body type. In 1912, separate classes were established for British and Russian Blues. After World War II, Scandinavian as well as British breeders began developing Russian Blues, crossing them with British Blue or Blue Point Siamese, which resulted in a new standard reflecting a more foreign body and a new voice. In 1965, some British breeders began returning the breed to its original conformation, and the next year, the standard was changed again.

Russian Blues are a challenge to breed because if the coat is correct, there is usually some other fault. And if a Blue lives in a warm climate, it loses its coat and becomes much lighter in colour.

SCOTTISH FOLD

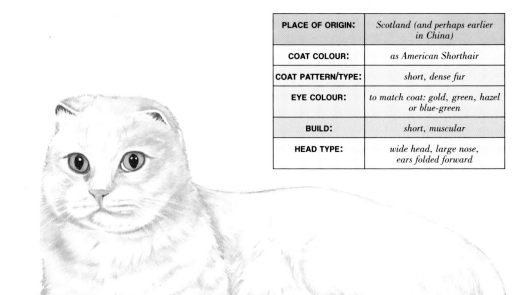

PLACE OF ORIGIN:	*Scotland (and perhaps earlier in China)*
COAT COLOUR:	*as American Shorthair*
COAT PATTERN/TYPE:	*short, dense fur*
EYE COLOUR:	*to match coat: gold, green, hazel or blue-green*
BUILD:	*short, muscular*
HEAD TYPE:	*wide head, large nose, ears folded forward*

White Scottish Fold

The first thing you notice about a Scottish Fold is that its ears are folded forward, giving the appearance of a cat wearing a close-fitting cap or one that perhaps doesn't want to hear what you are saying. Historical chronicles refer to a cat with forward-falling ears taken to Europe from China by an English sailor in the 1880s. It was greeted with interest because, until that time, all known cats in the world had erect ears.

Cats with forward ears resurfaced in 1961 on a farm in Perthshire, Scotland. A shepherd, William Ross, adopted one of the kittens, a white female named Snooks, and registered her. It is not known whether these twentieth-century cats had any connection to those in nineteenth-century China.

American and Australian organizations have given the Scottish Fold full recognition, but British and European groups have not – as they feel that the folded ear is undesirable because it could promote ear mites and impaired hearing. Most experts, however, say that the folded ears cause no discomfort or disability. Nevertheless, British breeders have had to register overseas, and now there are more Scottish Folds bred in the United States than in Britain. They were registered by the CFA in 1974 and received championship status in 1976.

Folded ears come from a single, dominant gene, but unfortunately they are sometimes linked with a deformity in which the legs and tail are thickened. The tail thickening was at first considered desirable, but because the leg thickening interfered with the normal gait, they are now regarded as undesirable traits.

The Scottish Fold should have a wide head, short neck, round eyes, large nose and flexible tail. The short, dense coat may be in 23 of the recognized colours of the American Shorthair: white, black, blue, red, cream, smoke, chinchilla, tabby and more. Eye colour, which should match the coat, can be gold, green, hazel or blue-green. Faults are erect ears, small head, and a thick, short or kinked tail.

A remarkable mouser, the Scottish Fold also hunts other small animals. Scottish Folds become attached to only one member of the household but enjoy the company of the whole. Folded ears cannot be detected on kittens until they are at least a month old.

SIAMESE

PLACE OF ORIGIN:	*Thailand*
COAT COLOUR:	*pale coat with darker points – seal, blue, chocolate and lilac*
COAT PATTERN/TYPE:	*points on mask, ears, legs, feet and tail; short, close-fitting fur*
EYE COLOUR:	*clear blue*
BUILD:	*medium-sized, lanky with long, slim hind legs slightly longer than front legs*
HEAD TYPE:	*long, triangular, with large ears*

Seal Point Siamese

One of the most popular breeds, the Siamese is also one of the most exotic-looking. It should be medium in size, lanky, with long, slim hind legs held slightly higher than the front. The head should be long and perfectly triangular from the tip of the nose to the tips of the large, pointed ears. The coat should be short, tight and close-fitting on the skin, with a very characteristic colour pattern of dark points against a pale coat. In the United States, the CFA recognizes four contrasting colour patterns:

● seal point, the earliest and most widespread colour, where the adult is beige with a seal-brown mask, ears, lower legs, feet and tail;

● blue point, which has the same beige-coloured body, but with blue-grey mask, ears, legs, feet and tail;

● chocolate point, with an ivory coat and milk-chocolate points;

● lilac point, with a glacial white coat and grey-pink points, including a lavender-pink nose.

All four patterns have clear blue, almond-shaped eyes, slanted towards the nose. At night their eyes shine red instead of the usual feline green. Faults are poor health; nasal obstruction; chin malformation; weak legs; crossed eyes; eyes of colours other than blue; excessive squinting; spots on the belly; too much brown on the head; wide cheeks and short muzzle; excessive sturdiness or thinness; short, hooked tail; and white feet.

The exact origins of Siamese are debatable, but they are known to have started in Siam (now Thailand). One story says they were bred by the kings of Siam and used as palace guards to jump on intruders from the walls. Another story claims that the sacred Siamese were engaged to guard a valuable vase (or Buddha's golden goblet, depending on the version). To protect it, they wrapped their tails around it and stared at it so earnestly that their eyes crossed.

A third story says that the dark mark on the back of the cat's neck (temple mark) was made when a god picked one of them up. Still another saga, explaining the kinked tail, says that the royal princesses of Siam kept their rings on the

Siamese kittens

cat's tail, which developed kinks to prevent them from falling off.

The King of Siam does bear some responsibility for increasing the Siamese's renown. In the 1880s he gave two Siamese cats to Owen Gould, English Consul-General in Bangkok. Gould took them to London and exhibited them at the Crystal Palace. In 1890 Siamese cats landed in America, probably as a gift from the King of Siam to an American friend. Soon after, they were priced as high as $1,000 each.

By 1892, the first Siamese breed standard had been written, describing it as 'curious and striking, of medium size, if weighty not showing bulk, as this would detract from the admired, svelte appearance. In type, in every particular the reverse of the ideal shorthaired domestic cat, and with properly preserved contrasts in colours, a very handsome animal, often distinguished by a kink in the tail.'

The kink eventually became a fault, but not before the first champion in Britain, complete with kink, had been named: Wankee born in Hong Kong in 1895. Some early cats also had the squinty, or crossed, eyes, which have been bred out.

Partly because of its personality, the Siamese became fashionable in the 1920s. Unfortunately, breeders could barely keep up with demand and took shortcuts that nearly wiped out the breed.

The Siamese line recovered, but was ravaged in the 1960s and '70s by feline leukemia virus. It has since recovered again.

Since the 1902 revision of the original standard, the Siamese has evolved into a more sleek and elegant animal than was the original version. The females reach adolescence sooner than those of other breeds and start calling at five months. Even so, they should not be mated until their ninth month. Born almost white, the kittens develop their final colouring gradually. Their eyes, too, change from light to brilliant blue.

Siamese are intelligent, loving, independent, talkative and sometimes unpredictable. They demand a great deal of attention and become jealous if they don't get it. They may become attached to one member of the household and take separation very hard. Although they won't come to heel, they enjoy walking on a leash.

SINGAPURA

PLACE OF ORIGIN:	*Singapore*
COAT COLOUR:	*ivory ticked with brown or bicolour of white with tabby markings*
COAT PATTERN/TYPE:	*smooth, close-lying fur*
EYE COLOUR:	*hazel, green or gold*
BUILD:	*small, muscular*
HEAD TYPE:	*round with short muzzle, very large eyes and pointed ears*

White Ticked with Tabby Singapura

As its name implies, the Singapura originated in Singapore, where it is the common cat of the streets and sewers. It leads a scrounging, tenuous existence on the small island because human residents there are not particularly fond of cats.

For centuries the small, muscular feline went virtually unnoticed as a distinct breed, until foreigners took an interest in its development. The first Singapura was exported from Singapore to the United States in the mid-1970s, and members of the breed were first shown in 1977. The CFA allows registration of the breed, while most other American organizations accept it for championship status.

Only ivory ticked with brown and a bicolour of white ticked with tabby markings have emerged outside of Singapore at this time. But the cat occurs in many colours and patterns on the island, and some of these can be expected to reach the outside world in the not-too-distant future.

The Singapura retains much from its deprived, streetwise heritage. It is smaller than other domestic cats, with males weighing no more than 2.7 kg (6 lb) and females attaining no more than 1.8 kg (4 lb). It is withdrawn and cautious towards new acquaintances, although it will warm towards anyone who demonstrates that no harm is intended. It reflects this attitude in a perpetually worried look on its face.

The cat sports a smooth, close-lying coat over a small, muscular body with legs of medium length and small narrow paws. Its tail is medium to long and quite straight. The head is round with a short muzzle, firm chin, large pointed ears and very large eyes that are slightly slanted.

Although the Singapura is a street cat by ancestry, it quickly adapts to any environment where it feels cared for. It can develop into an active, playful cat, curious about and involved in the family's every activity.

Owing to its recent 'discovery', the breed remains relatively rare. There is generally a waiting list for kittens, which are very slow to develop. They spend the entirety of their first four to five weeks of life in the nest box where they were born, which is of mutual benefit to both mother and kittens.

SNOWSHOE

PLACE OF ORIGIN:	*North America*
COAT COLOUR:	*seal point or blue point*
COAT PATTERN/TYPE:	*darker markings on legs, tail, face and ears; white paws*
EYE COLOUR:	*blue*
BUILD:	*medium to large, muscular*
HEAD TYPE:	*triangular with large, pointed ears*

Blue Point Snowshoe

The Snowshoe, so named for its white mittens, is the essence of a modern, manmade breed. It saw its beginnings in a natural mutation that resulted from the crossing of two Siamese cats in the mid-1960s, giving rise to a litter that included three female kittens with white feet. Without a strict breeding programme, such infrequent mutations could have remained the type's only occurrence.

Several American breeders, however, did take a fancy to these beautifully marked cats. They began their efforts by crossing bicolour American Shorthairs with Siamese having white feet, which produced a first generation that was in reality solid or bicolour Oriental Shorthair but registered as Snowshoes. The white-footed bicolours of that first generation were next crossed with Siamese, producing solid, bicolour solid, pointed and bicolour pointed cats. The bicolour pointed cats with white feet were then bred to other bicolour pointed cats to produce only bicolour pointed kittens, which were then bred as Snowshoe to Snowshoe.

Also called the Silver Lace because the white paws resemble those of the Birman, the Snowshoe retains the dark points of the Siamese on its legs, tail, face and ears. Only two varieties of colours are currently accepted for showing: seal point, which is yellowish to reddish brown with dark brown points, and blue point, which is bluish white with dark grey points. The eyes are blue. The CFA accepted the Snowshoe into championship status in 1983, but many other organizations have yet to recognize the breed.

A smooth, lustrous coat covers a medium to large, muscular body with medium legs and a medium to long tail. The head is triangular, but not delicate, with large, almond-shaped eyes that are slightly slanted and large, pointed ears.

The Snowshoe is highly people-oriented and will follow members of the family about the house in an ever-present fashion. It hates to be alone and needs a great deal of companionship and attention. Although it lives best as a strictly indoor cat, it remains active throughout its life. Its soft, delicate voice reveals the cat's loving nature.

Given its very recent origins as a breed, the Snowshoe remains relatively rare throughout the world.

SPHYNX

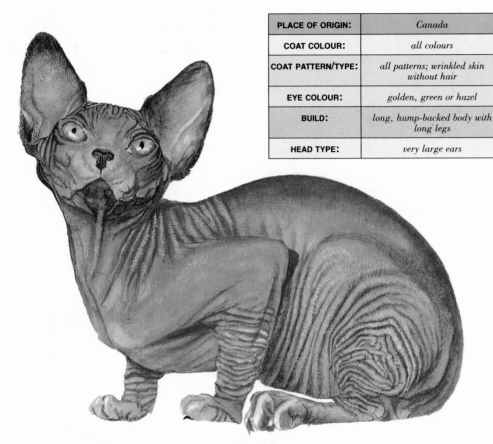

PLACE OF ORIGIN:	*Canada*
COAT COLOUR:	*all colours*
COAT PATTERN/TYPE:	*all patterns; wrinkled skin without hair*
EYE COLOUR:	*golden, green or hazel*
BUILD:	*long, hump-backed body with long legs*
HEAD TYPE:	*very large ears*

Blue Sphynx

When first viewing a Sphynx it is best to keep in mind the old adage, 'Beauty is in the eye of the beholder'. To many, this is the ugliest cat alive. But to its devotees, the tough, wrinkled, hairless skin and delicate, sweet expression have a beauty all their own.

Hairless kittens have occurred and continue to occur as infrequent mutations in the litters of many breeds. There is some evidence that the Aztec Indians of Central Mexico prized and encouraged such cats in their domestic breeds. The Mexican Hairless saw short-lived popularity in the late 1800s. But it was not until 1966 that a few breeders in Ontario, Canada, saw the potential for a new, distinctive, modern breed in the hairless kitten that appeared among an otherwise normal American Shorthair litter.

Efforts to perpetuate the breed, which is also nicknamed the Canadian hairless, are trying at best. The breed remains among the rarest on Earth. Crosses of Sphynx to Sphynx have not produced litters of hairless kittens.

The CFA has not recognized the Sphynx as a breed, although several smaller North American organizations have accepted it into championship status. Those organizations that do recognize the breed generally follow standards of a tough, wrinkled skin without hair; a delicate, sweet facial expression; enormous ears with indentations in their outer edges; large golden eyes (sometimes green or hazel); a long, humpbacked body with long legs; and a long, thin tail. All colours and patterns are generally accepted.

The Sphynx is a breed that requires plenty of care and attention. It hungers for as much physical contact as its owner can manage. It cannot exist outdoors, catching life-threatening colds in even the slightest draughts. It must eat frequently to maintain a relatively high body temperature (about 2°C or 4°F above that of other domestic cats) and because its body does not store significant amounts of fat.

TONKINESE

Natural Mink Tonkinese

PLACE OF ORIGIN:	*North America*
COAT COLOUR:	*natural mink, honey mink, champagne mink, blue mink, platinum mink*
COAT PATTERN/TYPE:	*with darker points as Siamese*
EYE COLOUR:	*rich blue-green*
BUILD:	*medium length with long legs*
HEAD TYPE:	*triangular with wide-set eyes and rounded ears*

Honey Mink Tonkinese

The Tonkinese is another deliberately created breed, but of longer history. From the 1950s through to the 1970s, North American breeders followed a breeding programme that crossed Siamese and Burmese. The hybrid result was a breed that retained some of the best traits of both its ancestral lines. It featured the dark coat of the Burmese with the visibly darker points of the Siamese.

'Tonks', as some refer to the cats, were registered with the Canadian Cat Association (CCA) in 1974 and the CFA in 1978. Championship status was conferred in 1984. Today, Tonkinese to Tonkinese crosses generally produce a litter that is one-half Tonkinese and one-quarter each of Siamese and Burmese.

The soft, lustrous coat of the Tonkinese looks and feels much like that of the mink and consequently its accepted colours have been given names that reflect this quality. The same colours in other breeds have not been awarded the 'mink' modifier. The recognized varieties are: natural mink, warm brown with darker points; honey mink, reddish brown with darker points; champagne mink, yellowish or greyish brown with light brown points; blue mink, bluish grey with darker points; and platinum mink, silver with darker points. Pale blue eyes are the accepted standard for all varieties.

The Tonkinese has a body of medium length with long legs (hind slightly longer than fore) and a long, tapering tail. Its triangular head features wide-set, slanted, almond-shaped eyes, a squared nose and medium-sized, rounded ears.

It is an extremely active and curious breed, which cannot be trusted near other small pets, such as birds and rodents, even when those other pets are 'safely' confined in their cages. The Tonkinese loves to jump and climb, and is quite willing to do so on trees or on shelves, furniture, curtains and the like. Plenty of exercise is essential to the well-being of this breed. It also thrives on a great deal of attention and tender care, and loves to greet visiting humans into its home.

LONGHAIR
BREEDS

Red Point Balinese

BALINESE

PLACE OF ORIGIN:	North America
COAT COLOUR:	chocolate, seal, blue or lilac points
COAT PATTERN/TYPE:	points on lighter background, as Siamese; long fur, but shorter and silkier than other longhaired breeds
EYE COLOUR:	blue
BUILD:	oriental, as Siamese
HEAD TYPE:	long, triangular

Chocolate Point Balinese

When Balinese kittens first appeared as spontaneous mutations – the result of a recessive gene characteristic in some American Siamese bloodlines – they were referred to as Longhaired Siamese. But as a few breeders began to develop further the longhaired coat in their cats, a new name emerged. The name 'Balinese' was borrowed from the native dancers on the island of Bali, whose graceful movements inspired one of the breeders to rename this lithe and elegant cat. American organizations began to recognize the breed in 1963 and it was appearing in shows in Europe by 1970.

The Balinese can appear in all of the myriad colours of its ancestral Siamese line, but the CFA currently recognizes just four for championship status: chocolate, seal, blue and lilac. The CFA considers red, tortie and lynx point

as Javanese, while some other organizations admit it as Balinese. The eyes in all varieties should be blue.

'Slim and dainty' best describes this breed, which features the Siamese body lines with a heavier, longer coat. Its fur, however, is not as thick as most other longhaired breeds, and it lacks a ruff about the neck and shoulders. Its coat is extremely soft and silky to the touch, and it tends not to mat and snarl as much as other longhaired cats. The medium-length tail ends in a thick, fluffy plume.

The Balinese is a lively, playful cat, which is characteristically persistent and clever in all its pursuits. Both its demeanour and its voice are quieter than those of its Siamese forebears. It craves, even demands, attention from a few select members of the family, whom it chooses on its own.

BIRMAN

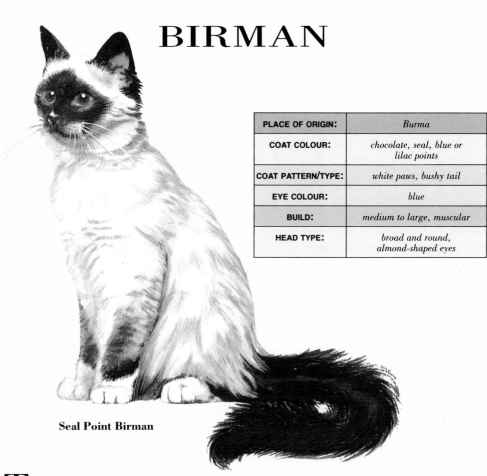

PLACE OF ORIGIN:	*Burma*
COAT COLOUR:	*chocolate, seal, blue or lilac points*
COAT PATTERN/TYPE:	*white paws, bushy tail*
EYE COLOUR:	*blue*
BUILD:	*medium to large, muscular*
HEAD TYPE:	*broad and round, almond-shaped eyes*

Seal Point Birman

The exact origins of the Birman breed are not known, but it is reasonable to assume that the feline has existed in much its present form in the South-east Asian republic of Burma for centuries. There it is known as the Sacred Cat of Burma and it occupies a special place in the religious lore of that country.

According to legend, the cats served as sentries in the Buddhist temples in ancient times. When invading hordes raided one of these sacred places – the temple of Lao-Tsun (a goddess of gold with eyes of blue gemstones) – they killed the head priest as he worshipped at the goddess's statue. The old priest's faithful cat, a pure white specimen, leapt on to the body of its dead master to protect it from further injury at the hands of the raiders. Immediately, its white body was transformed to gold, like that of the goddess, except for its paws, which remained white. Its face, ears, tail and legs took on the colour of the Earth and its previously yellow eyes turned to sapphire blue.

For seven days, the cat remained at its fallen master's side, refusing all food and preventing anyone from touching the body. Finally it died and its soul escorted the soul of the priest into the rewards of the afterlife. When the invaders finally left the temple, the other priests returned and gathered to select a new head priest. Their own white cats also returned, but now they all carried the markings of the dead cat. They encircled a young priest, who was then chosen as the new head priest.

The first 'modern' notice of the Birman breed was recorded in the final years of the nineteenth century by a British soldier on tour of duty through Burma. It became an established breed in France by 1925, recognized by the GCCF in 1966 and by the CFA in 1967.

The Birman is accepted in four colours, all having the characteristic white gloves: chocolate, which is gold-cream with warm chocolate points; seal, which is gold-cream with dark brown points; blue, which is gold-cream with blue-grey points; and lilac, which is white with pearl-grey points.

The Birman's medium-to-large body features large bones and a good musculature, with medium length, strong legs, short paws and a bushy tail. Its head is broad and round, and bears a strong muzzle, heavy whiskers, and almond-shaped eyes that are slightly slanted.

This tranquil breed is loving and faithful, even outgoing, towards humans who treat it gently and quietly. It lives best in a quiet, indoor environment, venturing outside only during the mildest of weathers. Its coat requires regular brushing and combing.

CYMRIC

PLACE OF ORIGIN:	*Isle of Man*
COAT COLOUR:	*various*
COAT PATTERN/TYPE:	*various; medium to long fur with heavy undercoat*
EYE COLOUR:	*to suit coat*
BUILD:	*long back legs, no tail, rounded rump*
HEAD TYPE:	*rounded with full cheeks, short nose, small ears*

Tortoiseshell Cymric

Cymric (pronounced kim-rik) is the Celtic word for Welsh. In this instance, it refers to the Isle of Man, where the ancestral Manx breed began.

The Cymric is a longhaired Manx that was first discovered in an otherwise normal Manx litter in Canada in the mid-1960s. The first Cymric kittens arose from carefully pedigreed Manx lines that bore no record of Persian influence. Breeders determined that the long fur was the result of recessive genetic traits, and began mating the new cats Cymric to Cymric, producing litters that were fully Cymric. Too much crossing of the tailless cats, however, also brings out lethal genetic deformities, and so tailed or stumpy-tailed cats must continue to be crossed into the line.

Although only a few North American organizations accept the Cymric (for showing but without championship status), the breed's standards have been established to pinpoint the essential feature of the Cymric, which is its total lack of a tail.

The Cymric's coat is medium to long – although always shorter than that of the Persian – with a heavy undercoat. The outer hairs are lustrous and smooth. All colours and patterns are accepted in the breed at this point.

Like its Manx progenitors, the Cymric is an intelligent and playful cat, generally docile but an excellent hunter and climber. It is friendly towards the entire family and anyone else who visits its home. The breed seems to do best when living exclusively indoors.

HIMALAYAN
(Colourpoint)

PLACE OF ORIGIN:	*United Kingdom/North America*
COAT COLOUR:	*seal, blue, chocolate, lilac, flame, tortie, blue-cream or lynx point*
COAT PATTERN/TYPE:	*markings as Siamese; coat as Persian but tail less thickly furred*
EYE COLOUR:	*deep blue*
BUILD:	*solid*
HEAD TYPE:	*round with round eyes and long whiskers*

**Flame Point
Himalayan**

After many decades of selective breeding, today's Himalayan features the unlikely combination of the Siamese pointed pattern on the long, flowing coat type of the Persian. The process that has given us this beautiful breed began in the mid-1920s, when a Swedish geneticist began crossing Siamese, Persian and Birman cats. His work was continued by geneticists at the Harvard Medical School through the mid-1930s, eventually producing the first Himalayan – named Debutante – in 1935. Although the scientists had named the first pointed longhair, they saw the work as nothing more than research without application for cat fanciers. With their results in hand, they were prepared to let the project drop.

But experimental breeding clubs, both in Great Britain and the United States, had learned of their work and had decided to continue development of the breed. The British breeders, who thought Debutante was too close to Siamese to be a breed of its own, received a tremendous boost to their efforts in 1947 when a woman offered them the use of her queen. This cat was a longhaired Siamese of unknown pedigree but remarkably close to the standards of the Persian. That cat's genes proved crucial in the further development of the breed. The GCCF recognized the breed in 1955, calling it a Colourpoint.

The Himalayan name, however, was conferred by the American breeders, who lagged behind their British counterparts by almost a decade. They borrowed the name from the Himalayan rabbit. The first Himalayans shown in the United States were unveiled in San Diego in 1957, the same year that the CFA and the American Cat Fancier's Association (ACFA) recognized the breed.

Himalayans are recognized in seal point, blue point, chocolate point, lilac point, flame point, tortie point, blue-cream point and lynx (tabby) point. Their coat is similar to that of the Persian, covering a solid body with medium-length legs and a straight tail that is not as thickly furred as that of the Persian. The head is round with plump features and extremely long whiskers.

The Himalayan is a very entrepreneurial cat, tending to decide on and develop its own activities. It is also affectionate and playful, taking pleasure in human-oriented activity. It is an efficient hunter, but not at all aggressive towards other cats.

JAVANESE

PLACE OF ORIGIN:	*North America*
COAT COLOUR:	*cream, red, tortie, lilac-cream or lynx points*
COAT PATTERN/TYPE:	*points on lighter background, as Siamese; long fur, but shorter and silkier than other longhaired breeds*
EYE COLOUR:	*blue*
BUILD:	*oriental, as Siamese*
HEAD TYPE:	*long, triangular*

Blue-Cream Point Javanese

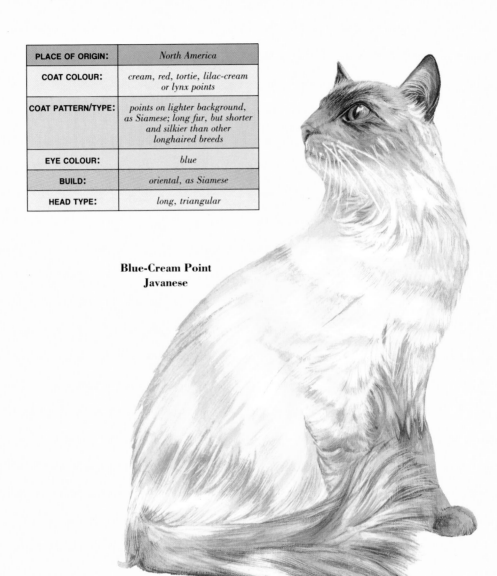

As breeders worked to develop the new Balinese breed, their crosses regularly produced a similar cat but of different colours than those they were trying for in the Balinese. The name of another Southeast Asian island – Java – was borrowed to describe what some saw as another new breed, the Javanese.

Different cat fanciers and organizations have chosen to view this cat in different ways: as a Colourpoint Shorthair with long hair, a Balinese in other Siamese colours, or a Siamese with long hair available in a great variety of colours. The varieties include: cream point, which is cream with pale yellow to reddish-yellow points; red point, cream with orangish-red points; tortie point, light brown to brownish orange with red and cream points; lilac-cream

points, snow white with pink-grey and cream points; and lynx point, any of these colours in a tabby pattern.

Except for its colour, the Javanese is a Balinese cat. It has the same soft, mink-like coat, short by comparison to other longhaired breeds, and lacks an undercoat and ruff. Like the Balinese, it is a thin and delicate cat that displays the typical Siamese body lines but under a heavier, longer coat. It has the same medium-length, plume-like tail.

The Javanese has an active, fun-loving nature, and is dedicated and intelligent in whatever it chooses to do. It has the same gentle voice and demeanour as the Balinese, as well as an intense longing for attention from a few family members of its own choosing.

KASHMIR

PLACE OF ORIGIN:	*North America*
COAT COLOUR:	*chocolate or lilac*
COAT PATTERN/TYPE:	*solid colour, silky, dense fur*
EYE COLOUR:	*copper in chocolate Kashmir; pale orange or copper in lilac Kashmir*
BUILD:	*solid with short legs and tail*
HEAD TYPE:	*wide and round with small rounded ears*

Lilac-Cream Kashmir

As the American breeders were working to develop the chocolate-point and lilac-point Himalayans, solid chocolate and solid lilac kittens occasionally turned up in the litters. When these cats were bred to each other, the offspring shared the pure-coloured coats. Some organizations viewed these cats as a new breed, naming them Kashmirs, but others saw them as a division of the Persian (CFA) or the Longhair (GCCF). They continue to cause disagreement today.

The chocolate Kashmir is medium to dark brown with copper eyes, while the lilac (also sometimes described as lavender) Kashmir is pinkish grey (actually a paler chocolate) with pale orange or copper eyes.

Apart from the solid colouring, all Himalayan characteristics have carried over into the Kashmir breed. The silky, dense fur covers a solid body with short legs, large round paws and a short bushy tail. The head is wide and round with round cheeks, a short nose, heavy whiskers and small ears with thick tufts.

Also like the Himalayan, the Kashmir is a well-behaved loving cat that is gentle towards humans and other cats but a great hunter of small prey. It enjoys some exercise space, but is content with a totally indoor existence. It also enjoys choosing and inventing its own activities.

MAINE COON CAT

PLACE OF ORIGIN:	*North America*
COAT COLOUR:	*various (see main text)*
COAT PATTERN/TYPE:	*silky, dense fur, longer on tail*
EYE COLOUR:	*green, gold or copper; white variety has blue eyes*
BUILD:	*large, heavy body*
HEAD TYPE:	*large and round with tufted ears and large eyes*

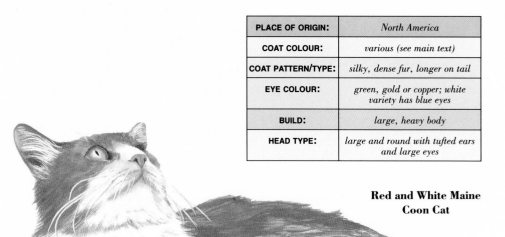

Red and White Maine Coon Cat

North America's answer to the Norwegian Forest Cat is the Maine Coon Cat. One explanation of the lineage of this distinctive breed even supposes that the Norwegian cat is the ancestor of the Maine cat, having come to the New World with ancient Norse explorers long before Columbus was born.

Other explanations abound. One states that the Maine Coon Cat is the result of matings between feral domestic cats and raccoons, which is how the cat gets its name, but is nonetheless genetically impossible. Another maintains that the Maine Coon has descended from cats sent to America by Marie Antoinette in preparation for escaping France before the Revolution caught up with her. Yet another says that the line was created by matings between shorthaired street cats brought to America by colonists in the seventeenth century and Angoras or Persians brought to the Continent by sailors in the 1800s.

This last explanation probably comes closest to the truth, but regardless of exact origin the fact remains that the Maine Coon Cat is the oldest natural breed in North America. It is generally acknowledged as a native of Maine and, in 1895, when the first professional cat show was held in North America, it won Best Cat honours.

The magnificent breed fell out of favour with much of the cat fancy when breeders began importing the refined Persians and Siamese, but since the 1950s has enjoyed a revival of interest. A Maine Coon Cat Club was organized among fanciers of the breed in 1953 and has annually chosen a Maine State Champion Coon Cat at a gathering in Skowhagan, Maine. The CFA granted championship status to the breed in 1976. The breed is allowed in 25 different colours and eight tabby combinations.

Weighing as much as 13.6kg (30 lb), the Maine Coon Cat is among the largest and heaviest of domestic cats. It sports a large, well-muscled body with a broad chest, medium-long legs, large heavily tufted paws and an enormous plume for a tail. Its head is large and round with well-developed facial features and generously tufted ears. The eyes are large, oval and wide-set, occurring in green, gold or copper. Only white members of the breed have blue eyes.

Despite its wild beginnings, the Maine Coon Cat of today is generally friendly towards all members of the household. It will, however, select one person for total devotion. It's a great hunter, but will adapt to indoor life as long as it is given ample outdoor exercise.

NORWEGIAN FOREST CAT

PLACE OF ORIGIN:	*Norway*
COAT COLOUR:	*any except Siamese types*
COAT PATTERN/TYPE:	*any except Siamese types; thick double coat with shorter undercoat*
EYE COLOUR:	*to suit coat*
BUILD:	*medium to long with stout legs and long tail*
HEAD TYPE:	*rounded with large round eyes and large ears*

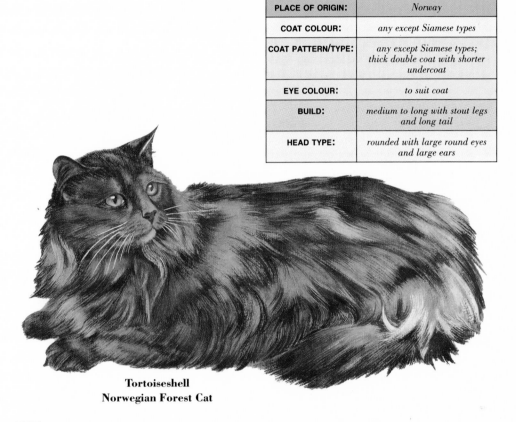

**Tortoiseshell
Norwegian Forest Cat**

The wild and free Norwegian Forest Cat evolved in the cold Norwegian forests, and was probably the result of crossings of shorthairs from southern Europe and longhairs from Asia Minor that were brought home by early Norwegian traders and explorers. Some bloodlines also include Persian, which found their way to Norway in the same manner, although the Norwegian Forest Cat is not a Persian hybrid. It is also a breed of long-standing, described both in ancient Norse mythology and (as a 'fairy cat') in the region's fables dating as far back as 1837. It is held in high esteem in its native land as a living monument to Norwegian culture.

Reflecting its wild, outdoor past, the breed exhibits a thick double coat that provides extremely effective insulation against the cold northern winters. A shorter, woolly undercoat holds in body warmth, while a longer outer coat provides resistance to snow and rain. The cat sheds almost its entire coat each summer, retaining long hair only on the tail, paws and ear tufts. The coat should be combed, not brushed, and only occasionally.

The cat reveals its heritage further in its love of the outdoors and in its inventive ability to teach itself many tasks, such as opening latches to let itself out and into the home. It also possesses some of the strongest claws among all domestic cats and is an excellent climber, even on rock surfaces.

Breeders began actively working with the Norwegian Forest Cat in the 1930s, and again after World War II and in the 1970s. The Federation Internationale Feline d'Europe recognized the breed in 1977, but it has yet to be recognized in the United States. All colour varieties, except the Siamese, are permitted.

The body is medium to long with medium, stout legs, a barrel chest and a long, heavily furred tail that is carried high. The head is rounded with large round eyes, large tufted ears and strong muzzle features.

Although it is well equipped to survive harsh weather in the outdoors, the Norwegian Forest Cat does adapt well to indoor life as long as it is has access to the outside. It can grow into an extremely loving and devoted companion of the entire family.

PERSIAN
(Longhair)

Known in Britain as the Longhair, the Persian embodies the stereotypical image of the pampered puss: super-soft locks of thick, luxurious fur; the aristocratic bearing; the self-satisfied facial expression. It is *the* pedigree cat for many casual observers.

An exact origin has not been pinpointed for the Persian; the earliest European records of any longhaired cats date from 1520. It appears that longhairs, most often referred to as Angoras, were introduced to the Continent at about that time. A sixteenth-century British manuscript described them as French cats because they made their way into England through France.

Given the very thick coat of both the Persian and Angora breeds, it is likely that both originated in the colder climes of northern Asia as wild cats that ventured into human settlements to escape the cold. In time, travellers and traders took these cats with them on their wanderings, and the cats eventually spread to Persia and Turkey.

Italian trader Pietro della Valle is credited with bringing the first longhaired cats out of Asia Minor to Europe in the late sixteenth century, but today's lines can be traced to cats brought to England directly from Persia and Turkey. From there the two breeds had developed along somewhat separate paths. The original Persians had heads that were both broader and rounder, ears that were smaller, bodies that were more muscular and fur that was thicker and fluffier than the Angoras.

The two were nearly recombined into one breed in the nineteenth century when crossbreeding resulted in the Persian characteristic proving dominant. The Angora was almost lost forever, until a revival of interest in the 1950s. In addition, much of Europe showed a decided preference for the Persian. The first official cat show in England, held in 1871, was dominated by the Persians, primarily of three types: white, black and blue. Several members of the ruling class added an official stamp of approval to the Persian. Queen Victoria, for example, owned a pair of blue Persians. The blue, probably resulting from crosses of blacks and whites, remains the most popular Persian today.

By the end of the nineteenth century, the Persian had made its way to North America, where breeders set about developing a cat with a heavier build and coat. At the same time, in Britain the white Persian had become a status symbol among the wealthy. Blue-eyed cats were particularly prized, despite the fact that many were born deaf.

The Atlantic continues to divide official opinion on this group of cats. In Britain, each colour variety is viewed as a separate breed. In the United States, all colours are considered varieties of the Persian breed, and some organizations go so far as to consider the Himalayans and Kashmirs as additional varieties.

In the United States, the CFA places each Persian into one of five divisions for showing purposes: solid, shaded, smoke/tabby, particoloured and point-restricted colours. In Britain, the Longhaired section is divided into nearly 50 different groups of colours and varieties, including Himalayan (known as Colourpoint in the UK).

All Persians share many common characteristics. They have a cobby body; short, thick legs; a magnificently furred tail ending in a large plume; round head and face; short, blunt nose; and large, round eyes. And, of course, there's that incredible fur, exceptionally full and thick, with a soft and woolly undercoat topped by longer guard hairs.

They are generally calm, peaceful and loving, but with a streak of determination and a strong desire for attention from their owners. Although they are not as active as some other breeds, they are generally efficient hunters and can be quite playful.

There are more than 30 varieties or breeds – depending upon which side of the Atlantic they are on – of Persians/Longhairs today. They include white, black, blue, red, peke-face, cream, several bicolours, tortoiseshell, black smoke, smoke tortoiseshell, blue smoke, cream shell cameo, cream shaded cameo, cream smoke cameo, red shell cameo, red shaded cameo, red smoke cameo, cameo tortie, cameo tabby, cream tabby, brown tabby, red tabby, silver tabby, blue tabby, calico (called tortie and white in Britain), pewter, chinchilla golden and shaded golden.

The white variety was the first longhaired cat to find its way into Europe. It was probably

White Persian

PLACE OF ORIGIN:	*northern Asia*
COAT COLOUR:	*various (see main text)*
COAT PATTERN/TYPE:	*various (see main text); thick fur with soft undercoat and longer guard hairs; plumed tail*
EYE COLOUR:	*various (see main text)*
BUILD:	*cobby with short, thick legs*
HEAD TYPE:	*round with short nose and large eyes*

of the Angora breed at first, but was replaced in the nineteenth century by the Persian. The blue Persian has been the most popular of the group since the days of Queen Victoria. It is equally popular with breeders because it can lend a near-perfect Persian body type into most breeding programmes.

Records of the black Persian date almost as far back as those of the white Persian. The pure black cat is a relatively rare thing; usually the coat will also carry some red or white as well. Dampness and sunlight also act against the black colour, giving it reddish or bleached tinges. Black Persians are more lively than most other Persians, although they can be just as loving.

The red Persian is an extremely rare cat. Most exhibit at least some off-red markings, often about the head. Reds were developed in England in the early 1900s. A controversial variety of the red Persian is the peke-face Persian. The name has been borrowed from the Pekinese dog because the cat has a face resembling that of the dog, with the short, snub nose and indentation between the eyes. The peke-face appears infrequently as a mutation in litters of red or red-tabby Persians. Some American breeders encourage the characteristic, but British organizations and some American ones too will not recognize the cat because its chief characteristic is actually a deformity that can cause health problems for the animal.

Accidental crossings of blue and red Persians resulted in a new cream Persian, which at first was discounted as 'spoiled' by British breeders. American fanciers took a different view and began to develop the cat.

A tortoiseshell Persian was created in the unintended matings of purebred Persians with non-pedigree shorthaired tortoiseshell cats. It remains a difficult cat to breed, necessarily involving crossings with bicolour males, and is both rare and expensive. Similar unintended

matings with 'moggie' tortoiseshell shorthairs are thought to have led to the first calico Persians, which resemble the printed cotton fabric of the same name. Because of the genetic linkages involved in producing this variety, most calico Persians are females and the few males are sterile. American and British stan-

Chinchilla Persian

dards differ over this variety, with the Americans desiring a cat that is white with coloured patches, and their British counterparts preferring the coloured areas to be dominant over the white. Calico Persians are called tortie and white Longhairs in Britain.

Tabby Persians are much more difficult to breed than tabby shorthaired breeds, because the longer hair tends to interfere with the patterns on the coat. However, some tabby Persians have been shown since the late 1800s.

The chinchilla Persian, developed from silver tabby Persians, gives a more dainty, delicate impression than most other Persians because of its fluffier fur. But the variety is no less sturdy than other members of the clan. Its coat is snow-white speckled with black on the head, back, flanks and tail. Its green eyes are outlined in black, appearing to have been framed in eyeliner make-up. Kittens begin life with dark streaks across their bodies, but lose these as they mature.

Two of the most recently developed varieties – the chinchilla golden Persian and shaded golden Persian – were developed as offshoots of chinchilla Persian breeding programmes.

When bicolour Persians first emerged on the cat show scene, they were lumped into the 'Any Other Colours' classification. However, fanciers pressed for a class of their own, which the British organizations granted, calling for patching that was exactly symmetrical. Over the years, that has been changed to allow all even patching. All solid colours in combination with white are recognized.

The pewter Persian, which is often confused with the chinchilla Persian, was developed in crossings of chinchilla, black and blue. The pewter tipping is much deeper than that of the chinchilla, rendering a darker coat in the tipped regions.

Cream Smoke Cameo Persian

Blue and White Bicolour Persian

Black Smoke Persian

The chinchilla golden Persian has a coat of light seal-brown tips on a cream undercoat. The shaded golden has heavier seal-brown tips on a cream undercoat.

Early crossings of black, blue and chinchilla Persians resulted in the first smoke Persians, which were included in British shows as early as the 1870s. The darker tipping – either black, blue or tortoiseshell – is so thick on a smoke Persian that the much lighter undercoat is virtually invisible until the cat moves.

Replacing the black speckling of the chinchilla Persian with cream, red, tabby or tortoiseshell are the various varieties of the cameo Persian. In addition, there are three major types of cameo, depending upon the amount of tipping on the coat: shell – short-coloured tips that give a hazy effect; shaded – longer coloured tips that shine; and smoke – coloured tips so long that they cover the white undercoat. The cameo Persian was developed through crossings of tortoiseshell and smoke Persians.

All Persians need daily grooming with comb and brush because of their dense coats. Even the smallest kink in the fur will cause the cat pain as it tugs against the skin. The thick, bushy tail is a particular target of fleas and ticks. Regular applications of baby powder or grooming chalk will also help to keep the hairs separated. Finally, regular bathing is needed to remove the excess oil before it builds up on the outer guard hairs.

Some Persians can tend towards obesity, which can then lead to cardiac problems, unless they are maintained on strict, veterinarian-prescribed diets. Also, the long hairs of the coat can be swallowed and lead to intestinal and respiratory problems, although daily brushing can help to prevent these.

Most Persian females have litters of two or three kittens, which are very delicate at birth. They require near-constant attention throughout their first four months. The female needs extra care and vitamins both during this period and all through her pregnancy.

RAGDOLL

PLACE OF ORIGIN:	*North America*
COAT COLOUR:	*seal, lilac, blue or chocolate points*
COAT PATTERN/TYPE:	*white paws and white on chest, underside, tail, neck and face; heavy coat, either long or semi-long*
EYE COLOUR:	*blue*
BUILD:	*large and heavy*
HEAD TYPE:	*wedge-shaped with broad features*

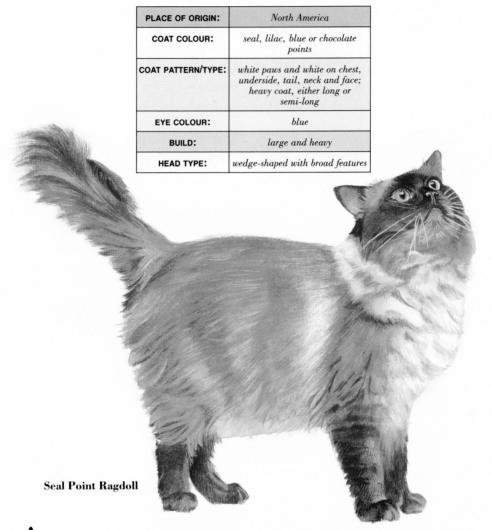

Seal Point Ragdoll

According to the lore surrounding the Ragdoll, the breed began with a single white Persian queen that was injured in a car accident just before she gave birth to a litter. Her kittens, or so the story goes, were born with an inability to feel pain or to fight other animals, and with a body that hangs limp when lifted.

While the three characteristics that mark the Ragdoll are described accurately, it would have been biologically impossible for them to have arisen from such an accident. Instead, the characteristics could only have been transferred genetically, and are believed to be the result of too-frequent selective breeding.

The first Ragdolls were actually produced by crossing white Persians with seal-point Birmans, and then mating the kittens with sable Burmese. Today, however, Ragdoll to Ragdoll crosses breed true. The resulting cat is large-bodied and heavy, with a broad chest, medium-length legs, large and heavily tufted paws, and a well-furred tail. The coat is heavy, either long or semi-long, and the head is wedge-shaped, with broad facial features. They are available in seal point, lilac point, blue point and chocolate point, each with white paws and white about the chest, underside, tail, neck and face.

The Ragdoll is a controversial breed because it is primarily distinguished by its limp and floppy nature when handled and its inability to feel pain. Only a few organizations recognize the breed, which remains relatively rare throughout the world.

Best with a quiet, calm owner, the Ragdoll is also happiest when leading a totally indoor existence. Its coat should be brushed regularly by hand or with a very light brush.

SOMALI

PLACE OF ORIGIN:	*North America*
COAT COLOUR:	*red and ruddy accepted; silver, blue and lilac also produced*
COAT PATTERN/TYPE:	*ticked fur, ruff, bushy tail*
EYE COLOUR:	*gold or green*
BUILD:	*long body and tail*
HEAD TYPE:	*rounded, wedge-shaped with large ears*

Red Somali

The Somali is a pleasantly wild-looking off-shoot of the Abyssinian that first appeared in litters of otherwise normal Abyssinians in the United States in the mid-1960s. The resulting kittens were longhaired Abyssinians, at first thought to be simple outcrosses to a longhaired breed. But research revealed that some bloodlines of the Abyssinian had indeed carried the recessive gene for long hair through several generations. With inbreeding that recessive gene was able to manifest itself in some lines, as long as the recessive longhaired gene was present in both parents.

The CFA granted championship status to the new breed in 1978, one year after it was officially presented at shows in Europe. Its first showings had come much earlier, in 1965, in Australia. Those organizations that do recognize the breed follow the same standard as that employed for the Abyssinian breed but with medium-to-long fur that is slightly ticked, a noticeable ruff, more heavily tufted ears and a bushy tail. Only red (red tipped with brown) and ruddy (orange-brown tipped with black) varieties are currently accepted, but breeders have been producing silver, blue and lilac for several years.

Although the Somali must be allowed outside during warmer months of the year, the cat is generally fearful of the cold and must be sheltered from winter weather. It is a skilled hunter, and a glutton for meat and giblets. Sometimes mistrustful in new and unfamiliar situations, the breed enjoys the company of those humans and other cats that it has come to know.

The Somali female gives a litter of only two or three very small kittens. They are very dark at first, and the distinctive ticking comes on to the coats only with maturity at about 18 months.

TIFFANY

PLACE OF ORIGIN:	*United Kingdom*
COAT COLOUR:	*sable*
COAT PATTERN/TYPE:	*solid colour with lighter ruff; long, silky fur*
EYE COLOUR:	*golden*
BUILD:	*medium-sized with long body*
HEAD TYPE:	*rounded on top with wide-set ears*

The Tiffany, actually a longhaired Burmese, was first produced in England in efforts to develop a solid chocolate Himalayan, which is now called a Kashmir. When Himalayans and Burmese were crossed, the litters contained several of the new longhaired breed.

The Tiffany, available only in sable with golden eyes, has the Burmese seal-brown coat but with a lighter, shimmering ruff. The coat is of medium length and quite smooth over the typical Burmese body. The face is somewhat fox-like with rounded eyes.

No organizations have yet recognized the Tiffany, which remains a relatively rare breed kept in existence by a handful of faithful breeders. It is a difficult breed to perpetuate because of the recessive longhaired gene involved; fewer longhaired kittens are born into each subsequent litter.

The Tiffany is a very playful cat, as long as the play is not too excited or strenuous. It is gentle, too, with a chirping, birdlike voice to match. Familiar creatures that share its home are generally the object of very vocal affection.

TURKISH ANGORA

PLACE OF ORIGIN:	*Turkey*
COAT COLOUR:	*white, blue, black, blue smoke, silver tabby, red tabby, bicolour or calico*
COAT PATTERN/TYPE:	*medium-length, silky fur without undercoat; plumed tail*
EYE COLOUR:	*to suit coat colour*
BUILD:	*fine bone structure*
HEAD TYPE:	*wedge-shaped with large ears*

Calico Turkish Angora

The Turkish Angora breed probably shares the same distant ancestors as the Persian, but the two breeds diverged when separate breeding populations became established in Turkey (Angora) and Persia (now Iran). The Angora was the first longhaired cat to be taken to Europe, first appearing in France and Italy in the sixteenth century. For a short time, British fanciers referred to it as the French cat because it was from that country that the breed entered England.

By the time of the first cat shows in the nineteenth century, however, the Persian was gaining preference over the Angora, which fell into rapid decline as a breed. As the twentieth century dawned, only a handful of the Angoras remained in Turkey. Outside Turkey, the bloodlines had been severely diluted through crossings with Persians.

After World War II, the Angora enjoyed a small resurgence in popularity. Given the old name of the city of Ankara – Angora – the breed was recognized by the CFA in the early 1970s, but only white specimens were accepted until 1978. Today it is accepted in blue, black, blue smoke, black smoke, silver tabby, red tabby, bicolour and calico, although white remains the most popular colour. Several American breeders are currently at work with the breed, using cats imported from the Ankara Zoo in Turkey, where the breed is the subject of a major preservation effort as the Turkish national cat.

The Angora has a long, slender body covered with medium-length, silky hair. It lacks the thick undercoat of its Persian cousin. It has a fine but strong bone structure; small, tufted paws; and a large, tapering but well-plumed tail. The head is wedge-shaped with roundish features and large, tufted ears.

It is a gentle, peaceful and well-behaved cat, perfectly suited to an indoor life. It can remain motionless for incredible lengths of time. Its fur is much easier to care for than that of the Persian, but still requires daily brushing and combing.

TURKISH VAN
(Turkish)

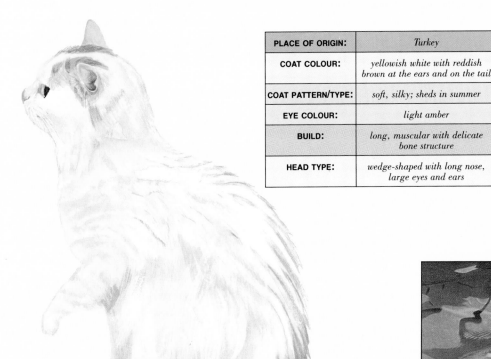

PLACE OF ORIGIN:	*Turkey*
COAT COLOUR:	*yellowish white with reddish brown at the ears and on the tail*
COAT PATTERN/TYPE:	*soft, silky; sheds in summer*
EYE COLOUR:	*light amber*
BUILD:	*long, muscular with delicate bone structure*
HEAD TYPE:	*wedge-shaped with long nose, large eyes and ears*

While British organizations do not recognize the Turkish Angora, American organizations do not recognize the Turkish Van (also called the Turkish). The latter cat is a true-breeding variety of the Angora that arose in the wintery Lake Van region of Turkey. Given its heritage, the Turkish Van loves swimming and splashing about in the water – the opposite reaction of the Angora.

In winter the soft, silky coat of the Turkish Van is quite similar to that of the Persian, but it is mostly shed in the summer. The coat is yellowish white, with reddish brown at the ears and on the tail, which is ringed with darker red.

The Turkish Van is a long, muscular cat, but with a delicate bone structure. The head is wedge-shaped with a long nose, large rounded eyes and large tufted ears that show pink on their insides. A loving cat, it eagerly spreads its affection throughout the family but gives most to a few chosen individuals. It exists best as an indoor cat with access to a garden or terrace. Daily brushing and combing, similar to that of the Persian, are recommended.

CAT ORGANIZATIONS

The following is a list of the main cat fancy organizations throughout the world.

American Cat Association, Inc.
8101 Katherine Ave
Panorama City CA 91402, USA

American Cat Fanciers' Association (ACFA)
PO Box 203
Point Lookout, MO 65726, USA

American Feline Society
41 Union Square W
New York, NY 10003, USA

American Humane Association
5351 S Roslyn St
Englewood, CO 80111, USA

American Society for the Prevention of Cruelty to Animals
441 E 92nd St
New York, NY 10028, USA

Canadian Cat Association (CCA)
14 Nelson St W, Suite 5
Brampton, Ontario L6X 1BY, Canada

Canadian Society for the Prevention of Cruelty to Animals
5214 Jean-Talon St W
Montreal, Quebec H4P 1X4, Canada

Cat Fanciers' Association (CFA)
PO Box 430
Red Bank, NJ 07701, USA

The Cat Fanciers' Club of South Africa
PO Box 783100
Sandton, 2146, SOUTH AFRICA

Cat Fanciers' Federation
2013 Elizabeth St
Schenectady, NY 12303, USA

Cat Survival Trust
Marlind Centre
Codicote Road
Welwyn, Hertfordshire AL6 9TV, UK

Cats Protection League
20 North St
Horsham, West Sussex RH12 1BN, UK

Co-ordinating Cat Council of Australia (CCC of A)
GPO Box 4317
Sydney, NSW 2001, AUSTRALIA

Crown Cat Fanciers' Association
1379 Tyler Park Drive
Louisville, KY 40204, USA

Fédération Internationale Féline (FIFE)
23 Doerhavelaan
Eindhoven 5644 BB, NETHERLANDS

Feline Advisory Bureau
350 Upper Richmond Road
Putney, London SW15 6TL, UK

Governing Council of the Associated Cat Clubs of
South Africa
45 Edison Drive
Meadowridge 7800, SOUTH AFRICA

Governing Council of the Cat Fancy (GCCF)
4-6 Penel Orlieu
Bridgwater, Somerset TA6 3PG, UK

The International Cat Association (TICA)
PO Box 2684
Harlinger, Tx 78551

Kensington Kitten and Neuter Cat Club
Fairmont
78 Highfield Ave
Aldershot, Hampshire, UK

Long Island Ocelot Club
PO Box 99542
Tacoma, WA 98499, USA

National Cat Club
The Laurels
Chesham Lane
Wendover, Buckinghamshire, UK

Royal Society for the Prevention of Cruelty to
Animals (RSPCA)
The Manor House
Causeway
Horsham, West Sussex RH12 1HG, UK

United Cat Federation
6621 Thornwood St
San Diego, CA 92111, USA

INDEX

Notes

1. All references are to cats, unless otherwise specified.
2. Page numbers in *italics* refer to captions.

PICTURE CREDITS

b = bottom; t = top; c = centre; l = left; r = right